Spring 1999 Edition

COLLECTOR'S VALUE GUIDE™

Ty® Beanie Babies®

Contents

Ty® Beanie Babies®

Front cover (left to right): Foreground – "Tiny™" – *Beanie Babies*®, "Millenium™" – *Beanie Babies*®,
"Kicks™" – *Beanie Babies*®
Background – "Mac™" – *Beanie Babies*®, "Hippie™" – *Beanie Babies*®
Top Inset – "Erin™" – *Beanie Buddies*®, "Erin™" – *Beanie Babies*®
Back cover (left to right): "Bongo™" – *Beanie Buddies*®, "Valentina™" – *Beanie Babies*®,
"Valentino™" – *Beanie Babies*®

Managing Editor:	Jeff Mahony	Art Director:	Joe T. Nguyen
Associate Editors:	Melissa A. Bennett	Production Supervisor:	Scott Sierakowski
	Jan Cronan	Senior Graphic Designer:	Krys Furman
	Gia C. Manalio	Graphic Designers:	Lance Doyle
	Paula Stuckart		Kimberly Eastman
Contributing Editor:	Mike Micciulla		Ryan Falis
Editorial Assistants:	Jennifer Filipek		Jason C. Jasch
	Nicole LeGard Lenderking		David S. Maloney
	Ren Messina		David Ten Eyck
	Joan C. Wheal		
Research Assistants:	Priscilla Berthiaume		
	Beth Hackett		
	Steven Shinkaruk		

ISBN 1-888914-49-1

CheckerBee PUBLISHING

(formerly Collectors' Publishing)
306 Industrial Park Road • Middletown, CT 06457

collectorbee.com

*S*ince their debut in 1994, Ty® *Beanie Babies®* have become one of the most popular collectibles of all-time and a household name worldwide. *Beanie Babies* news is breaking every day, creating a need for an accurate source of information to help collectors find out the truth about the huggable creatures and their values on the secondary market. The **Collector's Value Guide**™ **to Ty®** **Beanie Babies®** – now in its 6th edition – will guide you through every aspect of collecting; from the "Original Nine" *Beanie Babies* to the hottest new collectible line from Ty – *Beanie Buddies®*. Inside, you will find the most comprehensive and up-to-date information, including:

❀ **New January Releases And Retirements**

❀ **Large Color Photos Of All The *Beanie Babies*, *Beanie Buddies* And *Teenie Beanie Babies*™**

❀ How To Spot And Avoid Counterfeit *Beanie Babies*

❀ *Beanie Babies* Headlines From Across The Country

❀ **A Special New Feature On *Beanie Babies* And The Internet**

❀ **The Latest List Of The Ten Most Valuable *Beanie Babies***

❀ Detailed Information On Variations, Including New Versions Of "Batty," "Derby," "Iggy," "Mystic" and "Rainbow"

❀ A Guide To Ty Tags – Including New Tush Tags For *Beanie Babies* And *Beanie Buddies*

❀ More Winners From Our Dream Beanie Contest

❀ And Much, Much More!

*T*hey're on television, they're in the newspapers, they've taken over the Internet . . . they're even in baseball's Hall of Fame. In some form or another, *Beanie Babies* have made their way into mainstream American culture. Whether you're a die-hard collector or an innocent bystander who's stumbled onto the craze, *Beanie Babies* have become very much a part of our lives.

H. Ty Warner introduced the first nine *Beanie Babies* in 1994, but the story begins long before that. The now self-made millionaire began working in the stuffed animal business after attending college in Michigan. As a salesman for Dakin, he sold stuffed animals to specialty shops. Showing up in a Rolls Royce and dressed in a fur coat and top hat, customers couldn't help but listen to his sales pitch. In the early 1980s, he quit his job with Dakin and traveled overseas. Upon returning to the United States several years later, Ty Warner embarked on a journey that's taken him to the top of the toy industry at full speed.

Ty Warner's success began in 1986 when he created a "litter" of Himalayan cats. Almost immediately, collectors fell in love with them. After the business began to boom, Ty Inc. was created and enjoyed continued success with its cuddly, well-made plush animals.

In 1993, Ty Inc. introduced a new plush collection called *Attic Treasures*™ and, though no one knew it at the time, the best was yet to come. In late 1993, at trade show in Chicago, Warner introduced an exciting new line geared toward kids – *Beanie Babies*. The *Beanie Babies* were bean-bag animals that were purposely understuffed, small enough to fit into coat pockets and, most importantly, priced at a "kid-friendly" level.

When Ty Inc. retired three of the early *Beanie Babies* in 1995, suddenly collectors *had* to have them . . . and so the

phenomenon began. One of the things that keeps the momentum going today is that the incredibly high demand means that even current *Beanie Babies* are difficult to find in stores. Warner, who remains the president of the company, does not sell his *Beanie Babies* to large chain stores. Instead, he makes them available in small gift and specialty shops. Even these retailers have restrictions on how many of the *Beanie Babies* they are allowed to order.

Adding to the line's success, in 1997 *Beanie Babies* began showing up at professional sporting events – baseball first, then basketball, football and hockey. One *Beanie Baby* gained national attention in 1998 when New York Yankees' pitcher David Wells pitched a rare perfect game. "Valentino" happened to be at the right game at the right time and now he sits proudly beside Wells' cap in baseball's Hall of Fame.

Beanie Babies have also been used as a source of fundraising by many large organizations. In Canada, the Sports Celebrities Festival turned to "Maple" for help in raising money and awareness for the Canadian Special Olympics. The bear, who already sports the Canadian flag, also came with a special swing tag. The project was a huge

THERE'S MORE?

Yes! *Beanie Babies* and *Beanie Buddies* are only two of the fun plush products created by Ty.

Attic Treasures™ . . . jointed – and sometimes clothed – bears, dogs, cats and more, created to look like they're from the Victorian Era.

Pillow Pals™ . . . baby-friendly plush animals filled with special stuffing with an all-new colorful look for 1999.

Ty® Plush . . . a large collection of plush animals dating back to 1986 and separated into five major categories – Bears, Dogs, Cats, Country and Wildlife.

success and soon led to a similar promotion featuring "Valentino."

McDonald's also saw the marketing potential of the *Beanie Babies* and, before collectors knew it, they teamed with Ty to offer smaller versions of the popular toys. During the spring of 1997 and 1998, the fast-food chain offered *Teenie Beanie Babies* as the toy in their Happy Meals. The tiny plush animal and the actual meal each came in their own special bag. These bags and anything else related to the promotion, such as the advertising pins McDonald's employees wore on their shirts, have gained value on the secondary market. So will the *Teenie Beanie Babies* return sometime in 1999? Collectors can only hope the answer is "yes."

The Beanie Babies® Official Club™ kicked off in 1998, and has since been a huge success. By joining the club, you get special privileges and first-hand news only available to members. Perhaps the most popular feature of the new club was a royal blue bear named "Clubby," who was available exclusively to members in 1998. The premier edition club kit, known as the "Gold Kit," was retired in December 1998. But don't worry, Ty is coming out with a second club edition in early 1999. It won't be gold, but members will have their own benefits, and if

WHO'S WHO?

Since December 31, 1997, the "Iggy" and "Rainbow" issue has baffled collectors everywhere. But now it looks as though these two *Beanie Babies* have resolved their differences. It turns out that the two lizards were sporting the wrong fabric – not the wrong tags, as was originally reported.

IGGY™
1st - Tie-dye fabric without tongue
2nd - Tie-dye fabric with tongue
3rd - Blue fabric without tongue

RAINBOW™
1st - Blue fabric without tongue
2nd - Tie-dye fabric with tongue

you're a "Gold Kit Member" you will receive special benefits as well.

In the Fall of 1998, a new line joined the Ty family. The
Beanie Buddies had been hinted about quite a bit in the "Info
Beanie" diary on the Ty web site but, until the official
announcement at the end of September, no one knew
for sure what to expect. Made of a special material
called Tylon, these larger animals (about twice the
size of *Beanie Babies*) are extremely soft and easy to
fall in love with.

www.ty.com

There were nine designs in the "original" group of
releases and they had hardly made it to stores before their
production ceased. Apparently, it's a slow process to make
Tylon and once the lot ran out more quickly than expected,
more had to be produced. With 14 new releases for 1999
(and one surprise retirement), the *Beanie Buddies* will surely
make a big splash in the coming months. Who knows?
They may become the next big craze!

The *Beanie Babies* seem to be everywhere, yet nowhere
at the same time. And it is this scarcity that has made
Beanie Babies the hottest collectible
around. So, whether you consider it an
economic value to collect these
bean-filled animals, or you think it's
a great hobby, remember the reason
Ty Warner created them – to pro-
vide a fun, easy toy for kids of all
ages to enjoy!

Members Only

C heck out the late breaking headlines!

GLORY DAYS! *The Sporting News* magazine recently announced their 100 most powerful people in sports for 1998. Joining such heavyweights as Rupert Murdoch, the owner of Fox Broadcasting Co. (#1) and everyone's favorite (retired) athlete, Michael Jordan (#4); was "Glory" the *Beanie Baby*, who became a national celebrity at baseball's All-Star Game.

SHY GUY TY! Notoriously camera-shy Ty Warner was spotted in the December 1998 edition of *Vanity Fair* magazine. Included in the year-end "Hall Of Fame" section, Ty was featured "at the drawing board" in a picture by famed photographer, Annie Leibovitz. The pictorial spread also featured such 1998 luminaries as baseball slugger Mark McGwire and ex-White House intern Monica Lewinsky.

IS THERE A DOCTOR IN THE HOUSE? On January 7, 1999, Ty's *Beanie Buddies* made a special appearance on an episode of NBC's popular medical drama, *ER*. Prominently featured in the hospital's day care center were "Quackers," "Rover" and "Twigs." Maybe now that George Clooney is leaving the show, perhaps they're looking for some new leading men?

WELCOME TO THE WORLD! The octuplets born in early December 1998 to Nkem Chukwu in Houston, Texas were given *Beanie Babies* to keep them company as they were being treated at the hospital!

"I'LL TAKE 'A PROMOTIONAL SUCCESS' FOR $500, PLEASE, ALEX." The popular television game show *Jeopardy* recently posed this question (er, answer) during a "Final Jeopardy" round: "This most successful McDonald's promotion was run two times." Can you guess the answer?

IT'S THE CUSTOM.   United States customs officials are now searching for illegal or counterfeit *Beanie Babies* in all luggage on flights from Beijing, China.

SECONDARY MARKET VALUE MEAL!   With massive lines of people that contradicted the concept of "fast-food," the *Teenie Beanie Babies* promotion was a phenomenal success for McDonald's in 1997. So, in 1998, executives figured to do some market research and included coupons toward other McDonald's food purchases in some of the toys' protective packaging. However, the survey was ultimately not very successful because few people opened the plastic bags for fear of losing out on the potential secondary market value of the *Teenie Beanie Babies*!

SAVE UP THOSE FREQUENT FLYER MILES! If you're ever laid over at the airport in Pittsburgh, Pennsylvania, be sure to stop by the new "Ty-riffic" store. Opened in December 1998, the store is full of great Ty merchandise, as well as some really long lines.

WHO'S THAT BEAR?   A donation from Ty Inc. for over $8 million was presented in November to Paul Burrell, Fundraising and Events Manager for the Diana, Princess of Wales Memorial Fund. A promotional picture of the event made waves on the Internet when viewers noticed a larger-than-life "Princess."   This began speculation that a *Beanie Buddy* version of the popular bear was coming. The rumor didn't materialize with the New Year's Day announcement of new releases . . . but stay tuned!

CREATIVE SPELLING.   The 1999 Ty retailer order form features an alternative to the traditional spelling of tie-dye: "Ty-dye!"

*J*ust when you thought Ty Inc. had released about every animal imaginable, a diverse new group of winter *Beanie Babies* have been introduced! On New Year's Day, Ty announced 24 new *Beanie Babies*, including a variety of unique designs including a jellyfish, a baby chick and a stork. For bear lovers, there are eight exciting new bear designs and tie-dye fans are treated to three new releases.

BEANIE BABIES®

1999 SIGNATURE BEAR™

Ty Inc.'s *Beanie Babies* come from the heart, and perhaps there's no better proof than this adorable "1999 Signature Bear." Collectors are going to love this brown bear who has Ty Warner's signature ("*Ty*") stitched onto a bright red heart on his chest.

This bull terrier isn't as "ruff" as he looks. He'll actually be hard to resist when collectors see him in person with that big brown patch over his eye. One of three dogs released for the winter season, "Butch" promises to always greet you at the door when you come home after a busy day.

BUTCH™

EGGBERT™

"Eggbert" hasn't quite hatched yet but she is ready to join your collection all the same! You better remember to make room for her shell, too, as it doesn't look like she'll be leaving it any time soon!

Even though this little lamb can withstand the cold weather of winter with her heavy wool coat, she'd rather be somewhere nice and warm. With her big brown feet and her bright pink nose, collectors are sure to find "Ewey" quite cuddly.

EWEY™

The teddy bears seem to be a favorite among collectors and this new release is no exception! "Fuzz" is dressed in his best fur and wears a navy blue ribbon around his neck – he's hoping he'll impress you enough to add him to your personal collection.

FUZZ™

GERMANIA™

"Germania" the curly brown bear has joined the other national bears as a representative of Germany. This bear will only be available in Germany, therefore, his tag is in German. Adding to this cute bear's allure is that his date of birth (October 3) commemorates the reunification of East and West Germany which occurred on that date in 1990.

It seems as though mountain goats are always on the edge and "Goatee" is no different. She'll even prove it to you by climbing every mountain just to be in your collection. But you'll want her just for her looks – she's got brown horns and a "goatee" under her chin . . . could this be how she got her name?

GOATEE™

GOOCHY™

This pastel, tie-dyed jellyfish must be one of the most unusual of all the *Beanie Babies*. "Goochy" has lots of tentacles to feel his way around and unlike most jellyfish, he even has eyes so he can see the rest of his friends in your collection!

HIPPIE™

Does this colorful bunny belong with "Peace" and "Garcia," or the trio of bunnies who preceded him? Whatever the case may be, "Hippie" is just happy to be one of the lucky new releases waiting for you!

WHAT'S NEW FOR BEANIE BABIES®

HOPE™

This unique prayer bear based upon a popular bear in the *Ty Plush* collection has joined her *Beanie Babies* friends. "Hope" may turn out to be a very fitting name for this bear, as collectors will *hope* they can find her to add to their collections!

KICKS™

This action-packed bear comes just in time for the spring soccer season! "Kicks" is decked out in a vibrant green fabric and has a soccer ball stitched on his chest. With the sport gaining so much popularity, you can bet this team player is going to become a favorite among collectors, both young and old!

LUKE™

With his puppy-dog eyes and big floppy ears, who could resist this adorable black Lab? "Luke" promises to be your companion for life, standing up to his popular status of man's best friend.

MAC™

It's probably no accident that "Mac" the cardinal was released after a certain sports celebrity broke the most powerful record in baseball history. The bright red bird is one of three birds released this year and promises to be a hit with collectors . . . especially with those in St. Louis, perhaps?

MILLENIUM™

Everyone is preparing for it, even the folks at Ty. This bright bear is ready to ring in the new "Millenium" with all of his favorite collectors! Wearing the world on his chest with the year "2000" stitched underneath, "Millenium" is definitely ready to celebrate the historic turn of the century!

MOOCH™

Don't let the name fool you . . . this spider monkey is only after one thing – a home. If you give him a spot in your *Beanie Babies* collection, "Mooch" promises there will be no monkeying around!

NIBBLER™

This little white rabbit hops into 1999 as one of two new rabbits to be released. Be careful, "Nibbler" likes to eat anything she can find – maybe that's how she got her name!

NIBBLY™

Just like "Nibbler," this brown rabbit loves to eat. But all the food in the world won't make "Nibbly" as happy as joining her *Beanie Baby* friends in your collection.

PRICKLES™

This is one hedgehog you'll love to hug. Instead of sharp needles covering her body, "Prickles" has soft fabric that's hard to resist. Collectors are sure to find this unusual animal very sharp!

SAMMY™

Could there be another baseball hero in the collection? This pastel tie-dyed bear *cub* is sure to win the hearts of collectors and fans alike. Even though it's winter, "Sammy" loves being out of hibernation and can't wait

#1 BEAR™

LOOKING OUT FOR #1

To show his appreciation for the sales reps that have worked to make *Beanie Babies* today's number one collectible, Ty Warner issued this extremely limited bear. The tag features a special message for the reps and has the date of the sales conference (December 11-14, 1998) where "#1 Bear" was distributed. Most importantly, however, each of these special gifts was signed and numbered by Ty Warner, himself.

to join your collection. The only other place he'd rather be is the Windy City.

SCAT™

Don't let this cat know that her name means to go away. Like most cats, "Scat" will do just about anything to please her new owner. Her soft fur and pink whiskers makes her the "purrrrfect" addition to your collection.

SLIPPERY™

This new seal will slip by if you don't rescue him! "Slippery" wants you to take him out of the cold waters and let him join his cousin, "Seamore," in the warmth of your home.

"Stilts," the long-legged stork, is delivering bundles of joy this winter. He joins "Pinky" and "Stretch" as one of the tallest in the *Beanie Babies* collection. With his long red beak and legs, he's sure to make this delivery one of the best ever!

STILTS™

TINY™

He may be "Tiny," but he's got a great big heart. This bright-eyed chihuahua will do all sorts of tricks for treats. The best treat you could give him is a place in your collection.

This blushing fuchsia bear joins the collection just in time for Valentine's Day and is ready to share her love with any collector. What "Valentina" is really looking for though is her significant other . . . we know him as the recently-retired "Valentino!"

VALENTINA™

BEANIE BUDDIES®

In the Fall of 1998, Ty Inc. made big news by introducing a whole new line. The *Beanie Buddies* look just like their smaller *Beanie Baby* versions, with different fabric. It's a softer fabric called "Tylon" that's hard to resist!

There were nine founding members of the *Beanie Buddies* and this season, there are 14 new ones, including versions of some of the top ten most valuable *Beanie Babies*. So, which ones do you want?

BONGO™

"**Bongo**" has been going bananas since becoming a member of the *Beanie Buddies*. Now that he's bigger, he can swing from taller trees. What he's most excited about though is getting the chance to climb into your collection.

BUBBLES™

She's not the only fish in the sea of Ty, but she's the biggest. "**Bubbles**" is also the first fish from the *Beanie Babies* to join the *Beanie Buddies* . . . you'll want to scoop her up in your net the minute you see her!

CHILLY™

The "big chill" is back, and it's no wonder since his *Beanie Babies* look-alike is one of the most sought-after in the collection. Hopefully "**Chilly**" will be available longer than his smaller version, but there's no guarantee!

CHIP™

A "**Chip**" off the old block – that's what you'll think when you compare her with the *Beanie Babies* version. Even though this one *looks* like a copycat, she's got a mind of her own and can't wait to prowl into your collection.

ERIN™

Once green with envy, "Erin" is now thrilled to have joined her friends this winter as a *Beanie Buddy*. Collectors are going to want to keep an eye out for her. She may end up being as hard to find as the *Beanie Babies* version.

HIPPITY™

"Hippity" is hopping down the bunny trail, whether Easter is on its way or not. This mint green bunny loves being one of the new *Beanie Buddies* and is anxious to arrive in stores for you to buy.

PATTI™

As one of the first *Beanie Babies* ever produced, it's no surprise that "Patti" has quickly paddled her way into the *Beanie Buddies* collection. Her bright magenta color and yellow beak will be hard to miss when you're searching for the perfect companion.

PEKING™

This panda looks adorable next to his *Beanie Babies* friend with the same name (and color, and shape, and . . .). Even if the smaller version of "Peking" is already in your collection, don't miss the rush to get this one!

TO BE ANNOUNCED!

A MYSTERY!

While New Year's Day brought about a slew of retirements and new releases, there was something missing (at least in the Ty catalog, anyway!). Slipped in amongst the new releases, there was a shadowy figure staking claim to a spot in the *Beanie Buddies* line-up. The image is certainly that of the outline of a bear but the catalog gives little indication of anything more than that the mystery man (er, animal) will be announced soon! For more information on the newest *Beanie Buddies* release, watch our web site at www.collectorbee.com.

Don't get upset if you missed your chance to get "Pinky" before she retired on January 1, 1999. Her *Beanie Buddy* counterpart was released the same day, and promises to bring your collection to new heights.

PINKY™

SMOOCHY™

Pucker up, this "Smoochy" is a cutie! If you think he's cute in the *Beanie Baby* version, wait until you see him as a larger *Beanie Buddy*! Collectors will want to make sure they get their hands on both of these frogs!

SNORT™

If he snorts, it's only because he likes you – and that's no bull! "Snort" likes just about everybody, especially the collectors who add him to their collections.

SQUEALER™

It will be springtime soon and what's spring without baby pigs running around. Now that his *Beanie Baby* counterpart has retired, "Squealer" the *Beanie Buddy* is now the reigning king of the barnyard mud pits.

TRACKER™

It's no coincidence that "Tracker" found the *Beanie Buddies* list and added his name to it! Now, he can join his larger-sized friends as the second dog (after "Rover") in this new line.

WADDLE™

"Waddle" is ready to escape the frigid temperatures and keep warm in your collection. This adorable penguin loved being a *Beanie Baby* so much, the thought of not being a *Beanie Buddy* left him cold!

RETIREMENTS

*T*y announced new retirements *in advance* for the first time on their web site during December 1998. *Beanie Baby* fans were notified of the retirements via tricky crossword puzzles posted on the site from December 1st through the 12th. The advance warning gave collectors a chance to scoop up the soon-to-be retired designs before their official retirement on January 1, 1999. All told, there were 26 *Beanie Babies* (including many 1998 releases!) and one *Beanie Buddy* that retired. Here is a list of the January retirements with their animal type, style number and issue year.

JANUARY 1999 RETIREMENTS

1998 HOLIDAY TEDDY™	Bear	#4204	1998
ANTS™	Anteater	#4195	1998
BONGO™	Monkey	#4067	1995
CHOCOLATE™	Moose	#4015	1994
CLAUDE™	Crab	#4083	1997
CONGO™	Gorilla	#4160	1996
CURLY™	Bear	#4052	1996
DOBY™	Doberman	#4110	1997
DOTTY™	Dalmatian	#4100	1997
FETCH™	Golden Retriever	#4189	1998

JANUARY 1999 RETIREMENTS, cont.

FLEECE™	Lamb	#4125	1997
FRECKLES™	Leopard	#4066	1996
GLORY™	Bear	#4188	1998
NUTS™	Squirrel	#4114	1997
PINKY™	Flamingo	#4072	1995
PUMKIN'™	Pumpkin	#4205	1998
ROARY™	Lion	#4069	1997
SANTA™	Elf	#4203	1998
SCOOP™	Pelican	#4107	1996
SNIP™	Siamese Cat	#4120	1997
SPIKE™	Rhinoceros	#4060	1996
STINGER™	Scorpion	#4193	1998
TUFFY™	Terrier	#4108	1997
VALENTINO™	Bear	#4058	1995
WISE™	Owl	#4187	1998
ZERO™	Penguin	#4207	1998
TWIGS™ (*Beanie Buddies*®)	Giraffe	#9308	1998

Ty® Swing Tags And Tush Tags

𝒰 pon entering the world of *Beanie Babies*, collectors quickly become aware of the importance of the trademark heart-shaped tag. Although the tags on these miniature beanbag creatures come with instructions to remove them, complying may also remove the majority of the animal's secondary market value.

In order to attain the highest price on the secondary market, both of the tags on a *Beanie Baby* should be in mint condition. The **swing tag**, also referred to as the hang tag, is the paper, heart-shaped tag which is affixed with a plastic attachment to the animal. The **tush tag** is a smaller cloth tag near the animal's posterior. Ripped or wrinkled tags can significantly reduce the beanbag's value on the secondary market, sometimes making it difficult to re-sell.

Why are tags so important? By looking carefully at the tag, collectors can identify which "generation" it is and determine approximately when their piece was produced. *Beanie Babies* have had a total of five tags since the line's introduction in 1994 and pieces with older tags are generally worth more than their recent counterparts.

Generation 1

The Beanie Babies Collection
Brownie ™ style 4010
© 1993 Ty Inc. Oakbrook, IL. USA
All Rights Reserved. Caution:
Remove this tag before giving
toy to a child. For ages 5 and up.
Handmade in Korea.
Surface
Wash.

BEANIE BABIES® SWING TAGS

Generation 1 (Early 1994-Mid 1994):

These single sheet tags feature a single red heart with "ty" printed on the front in skinny lettering. The animal's name, style number, reference to "The Beanie Babies Collection" and company information all appear on the back.

Generation 2

The Beanie Babies Collection
© 1993 Ty Inc. Oakbrook IL. USA
All Rights Reserved, Caution:
Remove this tag before giving
toy to a child. For ages 3 and up.
Handmade in China
Surface
Wash.

Chilly ™ style 4012
to _____
from _____
with
love

Generation 2 (Mid 1994-Early 1995):

While the outside is identical to the first generation tag, this tag opens like a book. The inside contains the animal's name and style number, a "to/from/with love" section for gift giving, a reference to "The Beanie Babies Collection," plus care, cautionary and company information.

Generation 3

Generation 3 (Early 1995-Early 1996):
Unlike previous tags, the "ty" logo on this generation tag is fat and puffy. All of the same information is provided on the inside of the tag, with the addition of a trademark symbol and Ty's three corporate addresses.

The Beanie Babies ™ Collection
© Ty Inc.
Oakbrook IL. U.S.A.
© Ty UK Ltd.
Waterlooville, Hants
PO8 8HH
© Ty Deutschland
90008 Nürnberg
Handmade in China

Garcia ™ style 4051
to _____
from _____
with
love

Generation 4

Generation 4 (Early 1996-Late 1997):
A yellow star containing the words "Original Beanie Baby" was added to the front of this tag. Also, the inside of this tag underwent major format changes; as a poem and birthday were added for each animal, as well as the Ty web site address.

The Beanie Babies™ Collection
© Ty Inc.
Oakbrook IL. U.S.A.
© Ty UK Ltd.
Fareham, Hants
PO15 5TX
© Ty Deutschland
90008 Nürnberg
Handmade in China

Doodle™ style 4171
DATE OF BIRTH : 3 - 8 - 96
Listen closely to "cock-a-doodle-doo"
What's the rooster saying to you?
Hurry, wake up sleepy head
We have lots to do, get out of bed!
Visit our web page!!!
http://www.ty.com

Generation 5 (Late 1997-Current):
While the only change on the outside of the 5th generation tag is the typeface of the phrase "Original Beanie Baby," the inside of the tag is significantly different. The birthday is written out rather than abbreviated, while "http://" is removed from the Internet address. The piece's style number is deleted (it can be found in the last four digits of the UPC code), and the corporate offices of Ty UK and Ty Deutschland are consolidated as Ty Europe. Also, the name "Beanie Babies Collection" became registered (®).

Generation 5

The Beanie Babies Collection®
© Ty Inc.
Oakbrook, IL. U.S.A.
© Ty Europe Ltd.
Fareham, Hants
PO15 5TX, U.K.
© Ty Canada
Aurora, Ontario
Handmade in China

Pinky™
DATE OF BIRTH: February 13, 1995
Pinky loves the everglades
From the hottest pink she's made
With floppy legs and big orange beak
She's the Beanie that you seek !
www.ty.com

A New Generation?: In the summer of 1998, some *Beanie Babies* tags began appearing with slight differences. The writing in the star logo has a different font, making the word "Original" appear smaller and the letters of the word "Baby" closer together. The font used on the inside of the tag is larger and darker, as is the writing on the back of the tag. Also, in January 1999, the Ty Europe Ltd. address was changed to "Ty Europe, Gasport, Hampshire, U.K." While some collectors speculate that these changes could be the birth of a new generation, others insist that they are merely modifications to the current swing tag generation.

New Generation?

The Beanie Babies Collection®

®Ty Inc.
Oakbrook. IL, U.S.A.

®Ty Europe Ltd.
Fareham. Hants
PO15 5TX. U.K.

®Ty Canada
Aurora. Ontario

Handmade in China

1998 Holiday Teddy ™

DATE OF BIRTH : December 25. 1998

Dressed in his P.J's. and ready for bed
Hugs given, good nights said
This little Beanie will stay close at night
Ready for a hug at first morning light!

www.ty.com

BEANIE BABIES® TUSH TAGS

Version 1: The first *Beanie Babies* tush tags are white with black printing and list company and production information.

© 1993 TY INC.,
OAKBROOK IL, U.S.A.
ALL RIGHTS RESERVED
HAND MADE IN CHINA
SURFACE WASHABLE

ALL NEW MATERIAL
POLYESTER FIBER
& P.V.C. PELLETS
PA. REG #1965
FOR AGES 3 AND UP

Version 1

Version 2: The red heart Ty logo is added and the information on the tush tag is printed in red.

Version 3: This tag features the addition of the name of the animal below the Ty heart and "The Beanie Babies Collection™" above the heart.

HAND MADE IN CHINA
© 1993 TY INC.,
OAKBROOK IL, U.S.A.
SURFACE WASHABLE
ALL NEW MATERIAL
POLYESTER FIBER &
P.V.C. PELLETS
REG. NO PA - 1965(KR)
FOR AGES 3 AND UP
CE

The
Beanie Babies
Collection™

Quackers

HAND MADE IN CHINA
© 1995 TY INC.,
OAKBROOK IL, USA
SURFACE WASHABLE
ALL NEW MATERIAL
POLYESTER FIBER
& P.V.C. PELLETS CE
REG. NO PA. 1965(KR)

Version 2   Version 3

Version 4: This tush tag sports a small red star on the upper left-hand side of the Ty heart logo. On some tags, a clear sticker with the star was placed next to the Ty logo.

The
Beanie Babies
Collection™

★

Tuffy

HAND MADE IN CHINA
© 1996 TY INC,
OAKBROOK IL, USA
SURFACE WASHABLE
ALL NEW MATERIAL
POLYESTER FIBER
& P.V.C. PELLETS CE
REG. NO PA. 1965(KR)

The
Beanie Babies®
Collection™

★

Hissy™

HAND MADE IN CHINA
© 1997 TY INC,
OAKBROOK IL, USA
SURFACE WASHABLE
ALL NEW MATERIAL
POLYESTER FIBER
& P.V.C. PELLETS CE
REG. NO PA. 1965(KR)

Version 4   Version 5

Version 5: In late 1997, these tags began to appear with a registration mark (®) after "Beanie Babies" in the collection's name and a trademark (™) after the animal's name.

Version 6: These tags feature another slight change in trademark symbols. The registration mark in the collection's name moved from after "Beanie Babies" to after "Collection." Some of the recent tush tags have also noted a change to "P.E." pellets from "P.V.C."

Version 6   Mid-1998

Also, in mid-1998, a red stamp began to appear inside some *Beanie Babies'* tush tags. The stamp is an oval containing Chinese writing and numbers.

Version 7: Ty announced that all 1999 *Beanie Babies* would be produced with a hologram on the tush tag, as well as a red heart printed in disappearing ink.

BEANIE BUDDIES® SWING TAGS

Generation 1

Generation 1: So far, there is only one generation of swing tag for the *Beanie Buddies*. It's the same size as the *Beanie Babies* tags and, on the outside, looks like a *Beanie Baby* 5th generation swing tag (with the exception of the word "Buddy" instead of "Baby" in the yellow star). The inside of the tag has the name of the animal and a fact about its *Beanie Baby* counterpart.

BEANIE BUDDIES® TUSH TAGS

Version 1: The first *Beanie Buddies* tush tags are white with a red heart containing the word "ty" in white letters. The back of the tag gives the company name and fabric information in black writing.

Version 2: The newest *Beanie Buddies* have "The Beanie Buddies Collection®" written in red lettering above the heart. The back gives the company name and fabric information written in red.

Version 1   Version 2

𝒯n this section, you'll see just how valuable the *Beanie Babies* have become. Our "Top Ten" list ranks the *Beanie Babies* according to their secondary market value. Since the market is constantly fluctuating, the value of these pieces can change quickly. The most valuable pieces include *Beanie Babies* that retired quickly, rare variations and *Beanie Babies* that were never released to the general public. Are your *Beanie Babies* on the list?

PEANUT™ (Dark Blue)
Market Value: ③ – $5,000

The most valuable of all the *Beanie Babies* is the result of a factory error. Only about 2,000 pieces were made before the color was changed to light blue, making the darker "Peanut" a rare find!

BILLIONAIRE BEAR™
(Employee Bear, Special Swing Tag)
Market Value: $4,200

In celebration of the continued success of Ty Inc. in 1998, Ty Warner gave each of his employees TWO of these bears. That's a perk that collectors would die for!

BROWNIE™
Market Value: ① – $4,175

In "Brownie" form, he was available for a very short time. His name was changed soon after he was introduced, sending collectors rushing to find him, and making him very valuable.

NANA™
Market Value: ③ – $4,050

"Nana" shares much of the same history as "Brownie." His name was changed to "Bongo" just after he was introduced. Under his new name, he remained on the market until New Year's Day, 1999!

TEDDY™ (Violet, Employee Bear, No Swing Tag)
Market Value: $4,000

This bear has become one of the most valuable, although it was never for sale and has NO swing tag. A gift of appreciation from Ty Warner to his employees, it looks just like the violet "Teddy" and wears a red or green ribbon.

DERBY™ (No Star/Fine Mane)
Market Value:  – **$3,700**

"Derby" rode into the new year with yet another variation. But it's the first version of him, with a fine mane and no star, that collectors seek!

PINCHERS™ ("Punchers™" Swing Tag)
Market Value: – **$3,600**

This is an example of when a mistake can be a good thing (for collectors at least). Some first generation tags on this animal read "Punchers," instead of "Pinchers."

TEDDY™ (Brown, Old Face)
Market Value: – **$3,000**

When this adorable bear first arrived, his "old face" launched him into popularity. If a collector is "unlucky" enough to have a 2nd generation tag for this "Teddy," it's still valued at $2,800! That's some consolation prize!

CHILLY™
Market Value: – **$2,450**

The fact that it's almost impossible to keep a stuffed animal clean, especially a solid white one, is all the more reason why collectors will pay big dollars to add a mint condition "Chilly" to their collection.

HUMPHREY™
Market Value: – **$2,400**

With his long, floppy legs and big nose, this camel was often overlooked by collectors. When he became one of the first three *Beanie Babies* to be retired, his scarcity caused his popularity to soar!

HOW TO USE YOUR COLLECTOR'S VALUE GUIDE™

*T*here are five simple steps in determining the current market value of your *Beanie Babies* collection:

① Record the price paid and the date purchased for each *Beanie Babies* piece that you own in the allotted space.

② Use the swing tag generation chart on the right to help you identify the generation of your *Beanie Baby* tag (for more information on tag generations, see pages 20-23).

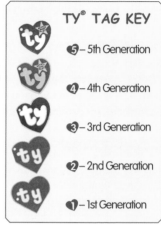

TY® TAG KEY

⑤ – 5th Generation

④ – 4th Generation

③ – 3rd Generation

② – 2nd Generation

① – 1st Generation

③ Find the value of the piece by looking at the dollar amount listed next to the corresponding heart. For current *Beanie Babies* with a fifth generation tag, fill in the current market value, which is usually the price you paid. If a piece's value is not established, it is listed as "N/E." Sports Promotion *Beanie Babies* are listed beginning on page 123 and are marked in the Value Guide with the appropriate symbol. *Beanie Buddies* begin on page 126, while the *Teenie Beanie Babies* section begins on page 139.

SPORTS PROMOTION BEANIE BABIES® KEY

🍁 Canadian Special Olympics

⚾ Major League Baseball

🏀 National Basketball Association

🏈 National Football League

🏒 National Hockey League

Women's National Basketball Association

④ Add the "Market Value" for each *Beanie Baby* you own and write the sum in the "Value Totals" box at the bottom of each page. Use a pencil so you can make changes as your collection grows.

⑤ Write in your totals from each Value Guide page on page 143-144 and add the sums together to get the "Grand Total" of your *Beanie Babies* collection.

COLLECTOR'S
VALUE GUIDE™

THE CHASE FOR BEANIE BABIES®

One of the most exciting aspects of collecting *Beanie Babies* is the thrill of the chase. While some *Beanie Babies* are easy to find at their original retail price of $5-$7, others are scarce and rise in value on the secondary market before they hit store shelves. Some hard to find current pieces and new releases are even more valuable than their retired friends.

In the Value Guide, all current *Beanie Babies* have been classified by the degree of difficulty in finding each piece at original retail price. Happy hunting!

DEGREE OF DIFFICULTY RATINGS

Just Released
Easy To Find
Moderate To Find
Hard To Find
Very Hard To Find
Impossible To Find

#1 Bear™
(exclusive Ty sales representative gift)

Bear · N/A
Issued: December 11-14, 1998
Not Available In Retail
Stores – Impossible To Find

Market Value:
Special Tag – N/E

1

NEW!

Dedication Appearing On Special Tag
In appreciation of selling over several Billion dollars in 1998 and achieving the industry ranking of #1 in Gift sales, #1 in Collectible sales, #1 in Cash register area sales, #1 in Markup %, I present to you This Signed and Numbered bear!

Birthdate: N/A
Price Paid: $_____
Date Purchased: _____
Tag Generation: _____

2

1997 Teddy™

Bear · #4200
Issued: October 1, 1997
Retired: December 31, 1997

Market Value:
④ – $60

Birthdate: December 25, 1996
Price Paid: $ _36.00_
Date Purchased: _May 1, 1999_
Tag Generation: _4_

Beanie Babies are special no doubt
All filled with love – inside and out
Wishes for fun times filled with joy
Ty's holiday teddy is a magical toy!

3

1998 Holiday Teddy™

Bear · #4204
Issued: September 30, 1998
Retired: January 1, 1999

Market Value:
⑤ – $50

Birthdate: December 25, 1998
Price Paid: $ _5.99_
Date Purchased: _Jan 29, 1999_
Tag Generation: _5_

Dressed in his PJ's, and ready for bed
Hugs given, good nights said
This little Beanie will stay close at night
Ready for a hug at first morning light!

Value Totals _____

COLLECTOR'S
VALUE GUIDE™

4

1999 Signature Bear™

Bear · #4228
Issued: January 1, 1999
Current – Just Released

NEW!

Market Value:
❺- $_____

No Poem_____
_____
_____

Birthdate: N/A
Price Paid: $ _5.99___
Date Purchased: _Feb. 18, 1999_
Tag Generation: _5_____

5

Ally™

Alligator · #4032
Issued: June 25, 1994
Retired: October 1, 1997

Market Value:
❹- $60
❸- $130
❷- $250
❶- $380

When Ally gets out of classes
    He wears a hat and dark glasses
    He plays bass in a street band
    He's the coolest gator in the land!

Birthdate: March 14, 1994
Price Paid: $_____
Date Purchased: _____
Tag Generation: _____

COLLECTOR'S
VALUE GUIDE™

Value
Totals _____

6

Ants™

Anteater · #4195
Issued: May 30, 1998
Retired: January 1, 1999

Market Value:
⑤- $13

Birthdate: November 7, 1997
Price Paid: $ 5.99
Date Purchased: June 1999
Tag Generation: 5

Most anteaters love to eat bugs
But this little fellow gives big hugs
He'd rather dine on apple pie
Than eat an ant or harm a fly!

7

Baldy™

Eagle · #4074
Issued: May 11, 1997
Retired: May 1, 1998

Market Value:
⑤- $22
④- $26

Birthdate: February 17, 1996
Price Paid: $ 10.00
Date Purchased: Feb. 13, 1999
Tag Generation: 5
E.

Hair on his head is quite scant
We suggest Baldy get a transplant
Watching over the land of the free
Hair in his eyes would make it hard to see!

Value
Totals _____

COLLECTOR'S
VALUE GUIDE™

8

Batty™   B

Bat · #4035
Issued: October 1, 1997
Current – Hard To Find
Retired March 31, 1999
Market Value:
A. Tie-dye
   (Oct. 98-Current)
   ⑤- $_____
B. Brown (Oct. 97–Oct. 98)
   ⑤- $10
   ④- $18

$5.00
May , 1998
5
E.
(A)

Bats may make some people jitter
Please don't be scared of this critter
If you're lonely or have nothing to do
This Beanie Baby would love to hug you!

Birthdate: October 29, 1996
Price Paid: $ *5.99*
Date Purchased: *Jan. 29, 1999*
Tag Generation: *5*

9

Beak™

Kiwi · #4211
Issued: September 30, 1998
Current – Moderate To Find

Market Value:
   ⑤- $_____

Isn't this just the funniest bird?
When we saw her, we said "how absurd"
Looks aren't everything, this we know
Her love for you, she's sure to show!

Birthdate: February 3, 1998
Price Paid: $ *5.99*
Date Purchased: *Jan. 11, 1999*
Tag Generation: *5*

COLLECTOR'S
VALUE GUIDE™

Value
Totals _____

10

Bernie™

St. Bernard · #4109
Issued: January 1, 1997
Retired: September 22, 1998

Market Value:
⑤- $11
④- $16

Birthdate: October 3, 1996
Price Paid: $ 6.00
Date Purchased: Jan. 8, 1999
Tag Generation: 5

This little dog can't wait to grow
To rescue people lost in the snow
Don't let him out – keep him on your shelf
He doesn't know how to rescue himself!

11

Bessie™

Cow · #4009
Issued: June 3, 1995
Retired: October 1, 1997

Market Value:
④- $68
③- $140

Birthdate: June 27, 1995
Price Paid: $_____
Date Purchased: _____
Tag Generation: _____

Bessie the cow likes to dance and sing
Because music is her favorite thing
Every night when you are counting sheep
She'll sing you a song to help you sleep!

Value
Totals _____

COLLECTOR'S
VALUE GUIDE™

12

Billionaire Bear™

(exclusive Ty employee gift)

Bear · N/A
Issued: October 10, 1998
Not Available In Retail
Stores – Impossible To Find

Market Value:
Special Tag – $4,200

Dedication Appearing On Special Tag
In recognition of value and
contributions in shipping over
a billion dollars since Jan '98,
I present to you this exclusive
signed bear!

Birthdate: N/A
Price Paid: $_____
Date Purchased: _____
Tag Generation: _____

13

Blackie™

Bear · #4011
Issued: June 25, 1994
Retired: September 15, 1998

Market Value:
5- $17
4- $20
3- $100
2- $235
1- $350

Living in a national park
He only played after dark
Then he met his friend Cubbie
Now they play when it's sunny!

Birthdate: July 15, 1994
Price Paid: $ 7.00
Date Purchased: Dec.31,1998
Tag Generation: 5

14

Blizzard™

Tiger · #4163
Issued: May 11, 1997
Retired: May 1, 1998

Market Value:
- 5 – $25
- 4 – $30

Birthdate: December 12, 1996
Price Paid: $_____
Date Purchased: _____
Tag Generation: _____

In the mountains, where it's snowy and cold
Lives a beautiful tiger, I've been told
Black and white, she's hard to compare
Of all the tigers, she is most rare!

15

Bones™

Dog · #4001
Issued: June 25, 1994
Retired: May 1, 1998

Market Value:
- 5 – $21
- 4 – $25
- 3 – $110
- 2 – $225
- 1 – $330

Birthdate: January 18, 1994
Price Paid: $ 5.99 trade
Date Purchased: Jan. 23, 1999
Tag Generation: 5

Bones is a dog that loves to chew
Chairs and tables and a smelly old shoe
"You're so destructive" all would shout
But that all stopped, when his teeth
Fell out!

Value
Totals _____

COLLECTOR'S
VALUE GUIDE™

Bongo™

(name changed from "Nana™")

Monkey · #4067
Issued: June 3, 1995
Retired: January 1, 1999

Market Value:
A. Tan Tail
   (June 95-Jan. 99)
   ⑤- $13
   ④- $17
   ③- $160
B. Brown Tail
   (Feb. 96–June 96)
   ④- $75
   ③- $155

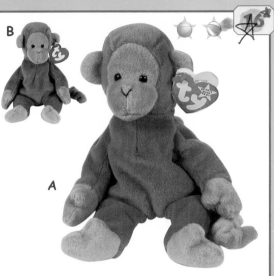

Bongo the monkey lives in a tree
  The happiest monkey you'll ever see
    In his spare time he plays the guitar
      One of these days he will be a big star!

Birthdate: August 17, 1995
Price Paid: $ _5.99_
Date Purchased: _Dec. 25, 1998_
Tag Generation: _5_

Britannia™

(exclusive to Great Britain)

Bear · #4601
Issued: December 31, 1997
Current – Impossible To Find

Market Value
(in U.S. market):
   ⑤- $425

Britannia the bear will sail the sea
  So she can be with you and me
    She's always sure to catch the tide
      And wear the Union Flag with pride

English money 40.00

Birthdate: December 15, 1997
Price Paid: $ _50.00_
Date Purchased: _June 1999_
Tag Generation: _5_

18

Bronty™

Brontosaurus · #4085
Issued: June 3, 1995
Retired: June 15, 1996

Market Value:
❸- $1,075

Birthdate: N/A
Price Paid: $_____
Date Purchased: _____
Tag Generation: _____

No Poem_____
_____
_____
_____

19

ORIGINAL NINE

Brownie™

(name changed to "Cubbie™")

Bear · #4010
Issued: January 8, 1994
Retired: 1994

Market Value:
❶- $4,175

Birthdate: N/A
Price Paid: $_____
Date Purchased: _____
Tag Generation: _____

No Poem_____
_____
_____
_____

Value
Totals _____

COLLECTOR'S
VALUE GUIDE™

Bruno™

20

Dog · #4183
Issued: December 31, 1997
Retired: September 18, 1998

Market Value:
⑤ – $11

Bruno the dog thinks he's a brute
But all the other Beanies think he's cute
He growls at his tail and runs in a ring
And everyone says, "Oh, how darling!"

Birthdate: September 9, 1997
Price Paid: $ 5.99
Date Purchased: Jan. 6, 1999
Tag Generation: 5

Bubbles™

21

Fish · #4078
Issued: June 3, 1995
Retired: May 11, 1997

Market Value:
④ – $170
③ – $235

All day long Bubbles likes to swim
She never gets tired of flapping her fins
Bubbles lived in a sea of blue
Now she is ready to come home with you!

Birthdate: July 2, 1995
Price Paid: $_____
Date Purchased: _____
Tag Generation: _____

22

Bucky™

Beaver · #4016
Issued: January 7, 1996
Retired: December 31, 1997

Market Value:
④- $42
③- $125

Birthdate: June 8, 1995
Price Paid: $_____
Date Purchased: _____
Tag Generation: _____

Bucky's teeth are as shiny as can be
Often used for cutting trees
He hides in his dam night and day
Maybe for you he will come out and play!

23

Bumble™

Bee · #4045
Issued: June 3, 1995
Retired: June 15, 1996

Market Value:
④- $645
③- $600

Birthdate: October 16, 1995
Price Paid: $_____
Date Purchased: _____
Tag Generation: _____

Bumble the bee will not sting you
It is only love that this bee will bring you
So don't be afraid to give this bee a hug
Because Bumble the bee is a love-bug.

Value
Totals _____

COLLECTOR'S
VALUE GUIDE™

Butch™

24

NEW!

Bull Terrier · #4227
Issued: January 1, 1999
Current – Just Released

Market Value:
⑤- $_____

Going to the pet shop to buy dog food
I ran into Butch in a good mood
"Come to the pet shop down the street"
"Be a good dog, I'll buy you a treat!"

Birthdate: October 2, 1998
Price Paid: $ _5.99_
Date Purchased: _Jan. 29, 1999_
Tag Generation: _5_

Canyon™

25

Cougar · #4212
Issued: September 30, 1998
Current – Moderate To Find

Market Value:
⑤- $_____

I climb rocks and really run fast
Try to catch me, it's a blast
Through the mountains, I used to roam
Now in your room, I'll call home!

Birthdate: May 29, 1998
Price Paid: $ _5.50_
Date Purchased: _Jan. 15, 1999_
Tag Generation: _5_

26

Caw™

Crow • #4071
Issued: June 3, 1995
Retired: June 15, 1996

Market Value:
❸ – $680

Birthdate: N/A
Price Paid: $_____
Date Purchased: _____
Tag Generation: _____

No Poem_____
_____
_____
_____

27

Chilly™

Polar Bear • #4012
Issued: June 25, 1994
Retired: January 7, 1996

Market Value:
❸ – $2,150
❷ – $2,300
❶ – $2,450

Birthdate: N/A
Price Paid: $_____
Date Purchased: _____
Tag Generation: _____

No Poem_____
_____
_____
_____

Value
Totals _____

COLLECTOR'S
VALUE GUIDE™

28

Chip™

Cat · #4121
Issued: May 11, 1997
Current – Easy To Find
Retired march 31, 1999
Market Value:
⑤- $_____
④- $14

Black and gold, brown and white
The shades of her coat are quite a sight
At mixing her colors she was a master
On anyone else it would be a disaster!

Birthdate: January 26, 1996
Price Paid: $ 5.99
Date Purchased: 4-8-99
Tag Generation: 5

29

Chocolate™

Moose · #4015
Issued: January 8, 1994
Retired: January 1, 1999

9
ORIGINAL NINE

Market Value:
⑤- $13
④- $16
❸- $145
❷- $270
❶- $400

Licorice, gum and peppermint candy
This moose always has these handy
There is one more thing he likes to eat
Can you guess his favorite sweet?

Birthdate: April 27, 1993
Price Paid: $ 4.99
Date Purchased: ① Sc 19, 1998
Tag Generation: 5
E = Me

30

Chops™

Lamb · #4019
Issued: January 7, 1996
Retired: January 1, 1997

Market Value:
❹ - $195
❸ - $260

Birthdate: May 3, 1996
Price Paid: $_____
Date Purchased: _____
Tag Generation: _____

Chops is a little lamb
This lamb you'll surely know
Because every path that you may take
This lamb is sure to go!

31

Claude™

Crab · #4083
Issued: May 11, 1997
Retired: January 1, 1999

Market Value:
❺ - $12
❹ - $17

Birthdate: September 3, 1996
Price Paid: $ 4.99
Date Purchased: Dec. 19, 1998
Tag Generation: 5

Claude the crab paints by the sea
A famous artist he hopes to be
But the tide came in and his paints fell
Now his art is on his shell!

Value Totals _____

COLLECTOR'S
VALUE GUIDE™

32

Clubby™
(exclusive to Beanie Babies®
Official Club™ members)

Bear · N/A
Issued: May 1, 1998
*To Be Retired: Orders Must Be
Postmarked By February 15, 1999*

Market Value:
$-$_____

PROUD

Wearing his club pin for all to see
He's a proud member like you and me
Made especially with you in mind
Clubby the bear is one of a kind!

Birthdate: July 7, 1998
Price Paid: $ 5.99
Date Purchased: Jan.23,1999
Tag Generation: 5
Me+ E.

33

Congo™

Gorilla · #4160
Issued: June 15, 1996
Retired: January 1, 1999

Market Value:
$-$12
$-$15

Black as the night and fierce is he
On the ground or in a tree
Strong and mighty as the Congo
He's related to our Bongo!

Birthdate: November 9, 1996
Price Paid: $ 5.99
Date Purchased: Dec.19,1998
Tag Generation: 5
E. Me

Value
Totals _____

43

34

Coral™

Fish · #4079
Issued: June 3, 1995
Retired: January 1, 1997

Market Value:
❹- $210
❸- $290

Birthdate: March 2, 1995
Price Paid: $_____
Date Purchased: _____
Tag Generation: _____

Coral is beautiful, as you know
Made of colors in the rainbow
Whether it's pink, yellow or blue
These colors were chosen just for you!

35

Crunch™

Shark · #4130
Issued: January 1, 1997
Retired: September 24, 1998

Market Value:
❺- $12
❹- $14

Birthdate: January 13, 1996
Price Paid: $_5.00_
Date Purchased: _Janu 11, 1999_
Tag Generation: _5_
_E._

What's for breakfast? What's for lunch?
Yum! Delicious! Munch, munch, munch!
He's eating everything by the bunch
That's the reason we named him Crunch!

Value
Totals _____

COLLECTOR'S
VALUE GUIDE™

Cubbie™

36

(name changed from "Brownie™")

Bear · #4010
Issued: January 8, 1994
Retired: December 31, 1997

9 ORIGINAL NINE

Market Value:
⑤- $32
④- $32
③- $145
②- $315
①- $450

Cubbie used to eat crackers and honey
And what happened to him was funny
He was stung by fourteen bees
Now Cubbie eats broccoli and cheese!

Birthdate: November 14, 1993
Price Paid: $_____
Date Purchased: _____
Tag Generation: _____

Curly™

37

Bear · #4052
Issued: June 15, 1996
Retired: January 1, 1999

Market Value:
⑤- $28
④- $34

A bear so cute with hair that's Curly
You will love and want him surely
To this bear always be true
He will be a friend to you!

Birthdate: April 12, 1996
Price Paid: $ _13.50_
Date Purchased: _Dec. 29, 1998_
Tag Generation: _5_

Value
Totals _____

38

Daisy™

Cow • #4006
Issued: June 25, 1994
Retired: September 15, 1998

Market Value:
- ⑤- $15
- ④- $20
- ③- $110
- ②- $230
- ①- $335

Birthdate: May 10, 1994
Price Paid: $ 10.00
Date Purchased: June 26, 1999
Tag Generation: 5

Daisy drinks milk each night
So her coat is shiny and bright
Milk is good for your hair and skin
What a way for your day to begin!

39

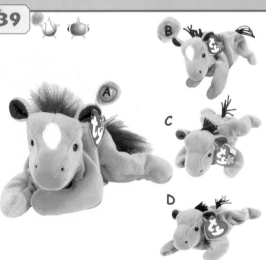

Derby™

Horse • #4008
Issued: June 3, 1995
Current – Very Hard To Find

Market Value:
A. Star/Fluffy Mane (Jan. 99
   -Current) ⑤- $_____
B. Star/Coarse Mane
   (Dec. 97-Jan. 99) ⑤- $10
C. No Star/Coarse Mane
   (Est. Late 95–Dec. 97)
   ④- $37 ③- $675
D. No Star/Fine Mane
   (Est. June 95–Late 95)
   ③- $3,700

Birthdate: September 16, 1995
Price Paid: $ 5.99
Date Purchased: Feb. 14, 1999
Tag Generation: 5

All the other horses used to tattle
Because Derby never wore his saddle
He left the stables, and the horses too
Just so Derby can be with you!

Value
Totals _____

COLLECTOR'S
VALUE GUIDE™

40

Digger™

Crab · #4027
Issued: June 25, 1994
Retired: May 11, 1997

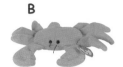

Market Value:
A. Red (June 95-May 97)
❹- $130
❸- $285
B. Orange (June 94–June 95)
❸- $800
❷- $880
❶- $975

B

A

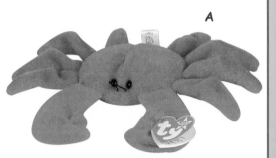

Digging in the sand and walking sideways
That's how Digger spends her days
Hard on the outside but sweet deep inside
Basking in the sun and riding the tide!

Birthdate: August 23, 1995
Price Paid: $_____
Date Purchased: _____
Tag Generation: _____

41

Doby™

Doberman · #4110
Issued: January 1, 1997
Retired: January 1, 1999

Market Value:
❺- $12
❹- $14

This dog is little but he has might
Keep him close when you sleep at night
He lays around with nothing to do
Until he sees it's time to protect you!

Birthdate: October 9, 1996
Price Paid: $ 4.99
Date Purchased: Dec. 6, 1998
Tag Generation: 5

COLLECTOR'S
VALUE GUIDE™

Value
Totals _____

42

Doodle™
(name changed to "Strut™")

Rooster · #4171
Issued: May 11, 1997
Retired: 1997

Market Value:
❹- $52

Birthdate: March 8, 1996
Price Paid: $ _3.50_
Date Purchased: _July 13, 1999_
Tag Generation: _5_

Listen closely to "cock-a-doodle-doo"
What's the rooster saying to you?
Hurry, wake up sleepy head
We have lots to do, get out of bed!

43

Dotty™

Dalmatian · #4100
Issued: May 11, 1997
Retired: January 1, 1999

Market Value:
❺- $12
❹- $16

Birthdate: October 17, 1996
Price Paid: $ _4.99_
Date Purchased: _Dec. 26, 1998_
Tag Generation: _5_

The Beanies all thought it was a big joke
While writing her tag, their ink pen broke
She got in the way, and got all spotty
So now the Beanies call her Dotty!

Value
Totals _____

COLLECTOR'S
VALUE GUIDE™

44

Early™

Robin • #4190
Issued: May 30, 1998
Current – Easy To Find

Market Value:
❤-$_____

Early is a red breasted robin
For a worm he'll soon be bobbin'
Always known as a sign of spring
This happy robin loves to sing!

Birthdate: February 20, 1997
or March 20, 1997
Price Paid: $ 5.99
Date Purchased: Dec. 26, 1998
Tag Generation: 5

45

Ears™

Rabbit • #4018
Issued: January 7, 1996
Retired: May 1, 1998

Market Value:
❤-$22
❹-$27
❸-$115

He's been eating carrots so long
Didn't understand what was wrong
Couldn't see the board during classes
Until the doctor gave him glasses!

Birthdate: April 18, 1995
Price Paid: $ 7.00
Date Purchased: April 18 1999
Tag Generation: 5

COLLECTOR'S
VALUE GUIDE™

Value
Totals _____

46

Echo™

Dolphin · #4180
Issued: May 11, 1997
Retired: May 1, 1998

Market Value:
🖐-$22
4️⃣-$26

Birthdate: December 21, 1996
Price Paid: $ _11.00_
Date Purchased: _Jun 26, 1999_
Tag Generation: _5_

Echo the dolphin lives in the sea
Playing with her friends, like you and me
Through the waves she echoes the sound
"I'm so glad to have you around!"

47

NEW!

Eggbert™

Chick · #4232
Issued: January 1, 1999
Current – Just Released

Market Value:
🖐-$_____

Birthdate: April 10, 1998
Price Paid: $ _5.99_
Date Purchased: _4-8-99_
Tag Generation: _5_
_Ed_

Cracking her shell taking a peek
Look, she's playing hide and seek
Ready or not, here I come
Take me home and have some fun!

Value
Totals _____

COLLECTOR'S
VALUE GUIDE™

Erin™

48

Bear · #4186
Issued: January 31, 1998
Current – Hard To Find

Market Value:
⑤- $_____

Named after the beautiful Emerald Isle
This Beanie Baby will make you smile,
A bit of luck, a pot of gold,
Light up the faces, both young and old!

Birthdate: March 17, 1997
Price Paid: $ *10.00*
Date Purchased: *Jan. 9, 1999*
Tag Generation: *5*

Ewey™

49

NEW!

Lamb · #4219
Issued: January 1, 1999
Current – Just Released

Market Value:
⑤- $_____

Needles and yarn, Ewey loves to knit
Making sweaters with perfect fit
Happy to make one for you and me
Showing off hers, for all to see!

Birthdate: March 1, 1998
Price Paid: $ *5.95*
Date Purchased: *3-19-99*
Tag Generation: _____

COLLECTOR'S
VALUE GUIDE™

Value
Totals _____

VALUE GUIDE — BEANIE BABIES®

50

Fetch™

Golden Retriever · #4189
Issued: May 30, 1998
Retired: January 1, 1999

Market Value:
⑤ – $18

Birthdate: February 4, 1997
Price Paid: $ _4.99_
Date Purchased: _Dec. 26, 1998_
Tag Generation: _5_

Fetch is alert at the crack of dawn
Walking through dew drops on the lawn
Always golden, loyal and true
This little puppy is the one for you!

51

Flash™

Dolphin · #4021
Issued: January 8, 1994
Retired: May 11, 1997

Market Value:
④ – $125
③ – $215
② – $350
① – $450

Birthdate: May 13, 1993
Price Paid: $_____
Date Purchased: _____
Tag Generation: _____

You know dolphins are a smart breed
Our friend Flash knows how to read
Splash the whale is the one who taught her
Although reading is difficult under the water!

Value
Totals _____

COLLECTOR'S
VALUE GUIDE™

52

Fleece™

Lamb · #4125
Issued: January 1, 1997
Retired: January 1, 1999

Market Value:
⑤-$12
④-$14

Fleece would like to sing a lullaby
But please be patient, she's rather shy
When you sleep, keep her by your ear
Her song will leave you nothing to fear.

Birthdate: March 21, 1996
Price Paid: $_____
Date Purchased: _____
Tag Generation: _____

53

Flip™

Cat · #4012
Issued: January 7, 1996
Retired: October 1, 1997

Market Value:
④-$38
③-$130

Flip the cat is an acrobat
She loves playing on her mat
This cat flips with such grace and flair
She can somersault in mid air!

Birthdate: February 28, 1995
Price Paid: $_____
Date Purchased: _____
Tag Generation: _____

Value
Totals _____

54

Floppity™

Bunny · #4118
Issued: January 1, 1997
Retired: May 1, 1998

Market Value:
⑤- $24
④- $29

Birthdate: May 28, 1996
Price Paid: $ 11.66
Date Purchased: 4-10-99
Tag Generation: 5

Floppity hops from here to there
Searching for eggs without a care
Lavender coat from head to toe
All dressed up and nowhere to go!

55

Flutter™

Butterfly · #4043
Issued: June 3, 1995
Retired: June 15, 1996

Market Value:
③- $1,075

Birthdate: N/A
Price Paid: $_____
Date Purchased: _____
Tag Generation: _____

No Poem_____
_____
_____
_____

Value
Totals _____

COLLECTOR'S
VALUE GUIDE™

56

Fortune™

Panda • #4196
Issued: May 30, 1998
Current – Moderate To Find

Market Value:
⑤- $_____

Nibbling on a bamboo tree
This little panda is hard to see
You're so lucky with this one you found
Only a few are still around!

Birthdate: December 6, 1997
Price Paid: $ 13.50
Date Purchased: Dec. 29, 1998
Tag Generation: 5

57

Freckles™

Leopard • #4066
Issued: June 15, 1996
Retired: January 1, 1999

Market Value:
⑤- $12
④- $16

From the trees he hunts prey
In the night and in the day
He's the king of camouflage
Look real close, he's no mirage!

Birthdate: June 3, 1996
or July 28, 1996
Price Paid: $ 5.99
Date Purchased: Dec. 15, 1998
Tag Generation: 5

58
NEW!

Fuzz™

Bear · #4237
Issued: January 1, 1999
Current – Just Released

Market Value:
⑤- $_____

Birthdate: July 23, 1998
Price Paid: $ _20.00_
Date Purchased: _april 9, 1999_
Tag Generation: _5_

Look closely at this handsome bear
His texture is really quite rare.
With golden highlights in his hair
He has class, style and flair!

59

Garcia™

Bear · #4051
Issued: January 7, 1996
Retired: May 11, 1997

Market Value:
④- $210
③- $280

Birthdate: August 1, 1995
Price Paid: $_____
Date Purchased: _____
Tag Generation: _____

The Beanies use to follow him around
Because Garcia traveled from town to town
He's pretty popular as you can see
Some even say he's legendary!

Value
Totals _____

COLLECTOR'S
VALUE GUIDE™

Germania™

(exclusive to Germany)

Bear · #4236
Issued: January 1, 1999
Current – Just Released

Market Value:
⑤- $_____

60

NEW!

> **Poem Translation**
> Unity and Justice and Freedom
> Is the song of German unity.
> All good little girls and boys
> Should love this little German bear.

Einigkeit und Recht und Freiheit
ist der Deutschen Einheistlied.
Allen Kindern brav und fein
soll dieser Bär das Liebste sein.

Geburtstag: Oktober 3, 1998
Price Paid: $_____
Date Purchased: _____
Tag Generation: _____

Gigi™

61

Poodle · #4191
Issued: May 30, 1998
Current – Easy To Find

Market Value:
⑤- $_____

Prancing and dancing all down the street
Thinking her hairdo is oh so neat
Always so careful in the wind and rain
She's a dog that is anything but plain!

Birthdate: April 7, 1997
Price Paid: $ 7.00
Date Purchased: Dec. 26, 1998
Tag Generation: 5

Value
Totals _____

62

Glory™

Bear • #4188
Issued: May 30, 1998
Retired: January 1, 1999

Market Value:
- $40

Birthdate: July 4, 1997
Price Paid: $ 20.00
Date Purchased: Dec. 26, 1998
Tag Generation: 5

Wearing the flag for all to see
Symbol of freedom for you and me
Red white and blue – Independence Day
Happy Birthday USA!

63

NEW!

Goatee™

Goat • #4235
Issued: January 1, 1999
Current – Just Released

Market Value:
- $_____

Birthdate: November 4, 1998
Price Paid: $ 5.99
Date Purchased: Jan. 13, 1999
Tag Generation: 5

Though she's hungry, she's in a good mood
Searching through garbage, tin cans for food
For Goatee the goat, it's not a big deal
Anything at all makes a fine meal!

Value
Totals _____

COLLECTOR'S
VALUE GUIDE™

64

Gobbles™

Turkey · #4034
Issued: October 1, 1997
Current - Easy To Find
Retired march 31, 1999
Market Value:
- ⑤- $_____
- ④- $20

Gobbles the turkey loves to eat
Once a year she has a feast
I have a secret I'd like to divulge
If she eats too much her tummy will bulge!

Birthdate: November 27, 1996
Price Paid: $ *5.00*
Date Purchased: *may ,1998*
Tag Generation: *5*

65

Goldie™

Goldfish · #4023
Issued: June 25, 1994
Retired: December 31, 1997

Market Value:
- ⑤- $50
- ④- $50
- ③- $132
- ②- $255
- ①- $405

She's got rhythm, she's got soul
What more to like in a fish bowl?
Through sound waves Goldie swam
Because this goldfish likes to jam!

Birthdate: November 14, 1994
Price Paid: $_____
Date Purchased: _____
Tag Generation: _____

Value
Totals _____

66

NEW!

Goochy™

Jellyfish • #4230
Issued: January 1, 1999
Current – Just Released

Market Value:
⑤- $_____

Birthdate: November 18, 1998
Price Paid: $_____ *gift*
Date Purchased: *April 17, 1999*
Tag Generation: ___5___

Swirl, swish, squirm and wiggle
Listen closely, hear him giggle
The most ticklish jellyfish you'll ever meet
Even though he has no feet!

67

Gracie™

Swan • #4126
Issued: January 1, 1997
Retired: May 1, 1998

Market Value:
⑤- $20
④- $24

Birthdate: June 17, 1996
Price Paid: $_____
Date Purchased: _____
Tag Generation: ___5___

As a duckling, she was confused,
Birds on the lake were quite amused.
Poking fun until she would cry,
Now the most beautiful swan at Ty!

Value
Totals _____

COLLECTOR'S
VALUE GUIDE™

68

Grunt™

Razorback · #4092
Issued: January 7, 1996
Retired: May 11, 1997

Market Value:
④ – $185
③ – $275

Some Beanies think Grunt is tough
No surprise, he's scary enough
But if you take him home you'll see
Grunt is the sweetest Beanie Baby!

Birthdate: July 19, '1995
Price Paid: $_____
Date Purchased: _____
Tag Generation: _____

69

Halo™

Angel · #4208
Issued: September 30, 1998
Current – Very Hard To Find

Market Value:
⑤ – $_____

When you sleep, I'm always here
Don't be afraid, I am near
Watching over you with lots of love
Your guardian angel from above!

Birthdate: August 31, 1998
Price Paid: $ 6.99
Date Purchased: Jan. 15, 1999
Tag Generation: 5

Value
Totals _____

70

B

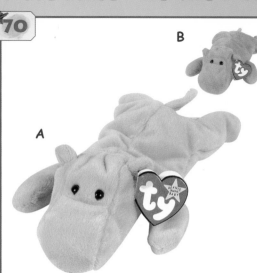

A

Happy™

Hippo · #4061
Issued: June 25, 1994
Retired: May 1, 1998

Market Value:
A. Lavender (June 95-May 98)
❺-$28
❹-$32
❸-$315
B. Gray (June 94–June 95)
❸-$800
❷-$870
❶-$950

Birthdate: February 25, 1994
Price Paid: $_____
Date Purchased: _____
Tag Generation: ___5___

Happy the Hippo loves to wade
In the river and in the shade
When Happy shoots water out of his snout
You know he's happy without a doubt!

71

NEW!

Hippie™

Bunny · #4218
Issued: January 1, 1999
Current - Just Released

Market Value:
❺-$_____

Birthdate: May 4, 1998
Price Paid: $_5.99___
Date Purchased: _Jan.15,1999_
Tag Generation: __5__

Hippie fell into the dye, they say
While coloring eggs, one spring day
From the tips of his ears, down to his toes
Colors of springtime, he proudly shows!

Value
Totals _____

COLLECTOR'S
VALUE GUIDE™

72

Hippity™

Bunny · #4119
Issued: January 1, 1997
Retired: May 1, 1998

Market Value:
- 5-$24
- 4-$29

Hippity is a cute little bunny
Dressed in green, he looks quite funny
Twitching his nose in the air
Sniffing a flower here and there!

Birthdate: June 1, 1996
Price Paid: $ _11.66_
Date Purchased: _4-10-99_
Tag Generation: _5_

73

Hissy™

Snake · #4185
Issued: December 31, 1997
Current - Easy To Find
Retired march 31 1999
Market Value:
- 5-$_____

Curled and coiled and ready to play
He waits for you patiently every day
He'll keep his best friend, but not his skin
And stay with you through thick and thin.

Birthdate: April 4, 1997
Price Paid: $ _5.00_
Date Purchased: _may, 1998_
Tag Generation: _5_
_E._

COLLECTOR'S
VALUE GUIDE™

Value
Totals _____

74

Hoot™

Owl · #4073
Issued: January 7, 1996
Retired: October 1, 1997

Market Value:
❹– $50
❸– $125

Birthdate: August 9, 1995
Price Paid: $_____
Date Purchased: _____
Tag Generation: _____

Late to bed, late to rise
Nevertheless, Hoot's quite wise
Studies by candlelight, nothing new
Like a president, do you know Whooo?

75

NEW!

Hope™

Bear · #4213
Issued: January 1, 1999
Current - Just Released

Market Value:
❺– $_____

Birthdate: March 23, 1998
Price Paid: $ 7.99 → (traded)
Date Purchased: Feb. 18, 1999
Tag Generation: 5

Every night when it's time for bed
Fold your hands and bow your head
An angelic face, a heart that's true
You have a friend to pray with you!

Value
Totals _____

COLLECTOR'S
VALUE GUIDE™

76

Hoppity™

Bunny · #4117
Issued: January 1, 1997
Retired: May 1, 1998

Market Value:
- 5 - $24
- 4 - $29

Hopscotch is what she likes to play
If you don't join in, she'll hop away
So play a game if you have the time,
She likes to play, rain or shine!

Birthdate: April 3, 1996
Price Paid: $ 11.66
Date Purchased: 4-10-99
Tag Generation: 5

77

Humphrey™

Camel · #4060
Issued: June 25, 1994
Retired: June 15, 1995

Market Value:
- 3 - $2,000
- 2 - $2,100
- 1 - $2,400

No Poem_____
_____
_____
_____

Birthdate: N/A
Price Paid: $_____
Date Purchased: _____
Tag Generation: _____

78

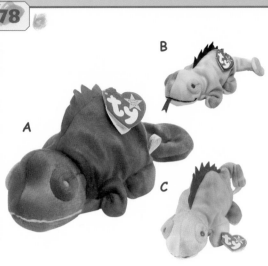

Iggy™

Iguana · #4038
Issued: December 31, 1997
Current – Easy To Find
Retired March 31, 1999
Market Value:
A. Blue/No Tongue
   (Mid 98-Current)
   ⑤- $_____
B. Tie-dye/With Tongue
   (June 98-Mid 98)
   ⑤- $15
C. Tie-dye/No Tongue
   (Dec. 97-June 98)
   ⑤- $20

Birthdate: August 12, 1997
Price Paid: $ *5.99*
Date Purchased: *Nov. 1997*
Tag Generation: *5*
E.

Sitting on a rock, basking in the sun
Is this iguana's idea of fun
Towel and glasses, book and beach chair
His life is so perfect without a care!

79

Inch™

Inchworm · #4044
Issued: June 3, 1995
Retired: May 1, 1998

Market Value:
A. Yarn Antennas
   (Est. Mid 96-May 98)
   ⑤- $25
   ④- $32
B. Felt Antennas
   (Est. June 95-Mid 96)
   ④- $180
   ③- $195

Birthdate: September 3, 1995
Price Paid: $_____
Date Purchased: _____
Tag Generation: *H*

Inch the worm is a friend of mine
He goes so slow all the time
Inching around from here to there
Traveling the world without a care!

Value
Totals _____

COLLECTOR'S
VALUE GUIDE™

80

Inky™

Octopus · #4028
Issued: June 25, 1994
Retired: May 1, 1998

Market Value:
A. Pink (June 95-May 98)
⑤-$36 ④-$42 ③-$290
B. Tan With Mouth
(Sept. 94–June 95)
③-$695 ②-$755
C. Tan Without Mouth
(June 94–Sept. 94)
②-$850 ①-$900

B

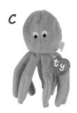
C

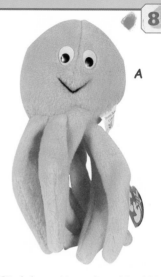
A

Inky's head is big and round
As he swims he makes no sound
If you need a hand, don't hesitate
Inky can help because he has eight!

Birthdate: November 29, 1994
Price Paid: $ 12.00
Date Purchased: april 18, 1999
Tag Generation: 5

81

Jabber™

Parrot · #4197
Issued: May 30, 1998
Current – Easy To Find

Market Value:
⑤-$_____

Teaching Jabber to move his beak
A large vocabulary he now can speak
Jabber will repeat what you say
Teach him a new word everyday!

Birthdate: October 10, 1997
Price Paid: $ 5.99
Date Purchased: Dec. 26, 1999
Tag Generation: 5

82

Jake™

Mallard Duck · #4199
Issued: May 30, 1998
Current – Easy To Find

Market Value:
⑤- $_____

Birthdate: April 16, 1997
Price Paid: $ 5.95
Date Purchased: Jan. 13, 1999
Tag Generation: 5

Jake the drake likes to splash in a puddle
Take him home and give him a cuddle
Quack, Quack, Quack, he will say
He's so glad you're here to play!

83

Jolly™

Walrus · #4082
Issued: May 11, 1997
Retired: May 1, 1998

Market Value:
⑤- $23
④- $27

Birthdate: December 2, 1996
Price Paid: $_____
Date Purchased: _____
Tag Generation: _____

Jolly the walrus is not very serious
He laughs and laughs until he's delirious
He often reminds me of my dad
Always happy, never sad!

Value
Totals _____

COLLECTOR'S
VALUE GUIDE™

Kicks™

84

NEW!

Bear • #4229
Issued: January 1, 1999
Current – Just Released

Market Value:
⑤- $_____

The world cup is his dream
Kicks the bear is the best on his team
He hopes that one day he'll be the pick
First he needs to improve his kick!

Birthdate: August 16, 1998
Price Paid: $ 5.99
Date Purchased: Jan. 30, 1999
Tag Generation: 5

Kiwi™

85

Toucan • #4070
Issued: June 3, 1995
Retired: January 1, 1997

Market Value:
④- $190
③- $270

Kiwi waits for the April showers
Watching a garden bloom with flowers
There trees grow with fruit that's sweet
I'm sure you'll guess his favorite treat!

Birthdate: September 16, 1995
Price Paid: $_____
Date Purchased: _____
Tag Generation: _____

Value
Totals _____

90

B

A

Lizzy™

Lizard · #4033
Issued: June 3, 1995
Retired: December 31, 1997

Market Value:
A. Blue (Jan. 96-Dec. 97)
⑤- $35
④- $35
③- $340
B. Tie-dye (June 95–Jan. 96)
③- $1,175

Birthdate: May 11, 1995
Price Paid: $ 16.66
Date Purchased: Feb. 13, 1999
Tag Generation: E

Lizzy loves Legs the frog
She hides with him under logs
Both of them search for flies
Underneath the clear blue skies!

91

Loosy™

Goose · #4206
Issued: September 30, 1998
Current – Moderate To Find

Market Value:
⑤- $_____

Birthdate: March 29, 1998
Price Paid: $ 4.95
Date Purchased: Jan. 13, 1999
Tag Generation: 5

A tale has been told
Of a goose that laid gold
But try as she might
Loosy's eggs are just white!

Value
Totals _____

COLLECTOR'S
VALUE GUIDE™

92

Lucky™

B

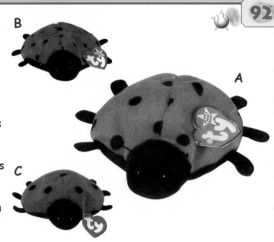

A

C

Ladybug · #4040
Issued: June 25, 1994
Retired: May 1, 1998

Market Value:
A. Approx. 11 Printed Spots
(Feb. 96-May 98)
5-$28 **4**-$33
B. Approx. 21 Printed Spots
(Est. Mid 96–Late 96)
4-$600
C. Approx. 7 Felt Glued-On
Spots (June 94–Feb. 96)
3-$225 **2**-$360
1-$450

Lucky the lady bug loves the lotto
"Someone must win" that's her motto
But save your dimes and even a penny
Don't spend on the lotto and
You'll have many!

Birthdate: May 1, 1995
Price Paid: $ _10.00_
Date Purchased: _Feb. 13, 1999_
Tag Generation: _5_

93

NEW!

Luke™

Black Lab · #4214
Issued: January 1, 1999
Current – Just Released

Market Value:
5-$_____

After chewing on your favorite shoes
Luke gets tired, takes a snooze
Who wouldn't love a puppy like this?
Give him a hug, he'll give you a kiss!

Birthdate: June 15, 1998
Price Paid: $ _5.99_
Date Purchased: _Jan. 15, 1999_
Tag Generation: _5_

Value
Totals _____

94

NEW!

Mac™

Cardinal · #4225
Issued: January 1, 1999
Current – Just Released

Market Value:
⑤- $_____

Birthdate: June 10, 1998
Price Paid: $ *5.50*
Date Purchased: *Jan. 3, 1999*
Tag Generation: *5*

Mac tries hard to prove he's the best
Swinging his bat harder than the rest
Breaking records, enjoying the game
Hitting home runs is his claim to fame!

95

B

A

Magic™

Dragon · #4088
Issued: June 3, 1995
Retired: December 31, 1997

Market Value:
A. Pale Pink Thread
(June 95-Dec. 97)
④- $55
❸- $155
B. Hot Pink Thread
(Est. Mid 96–Early 97)
④- $90

Birthdate: September 5, 1995
Price Paid: $_____
Date Purchased: _____
Tag Generation: _____

Magic the dragon lives in a dream
The most beautiful that you have ever seen
Through magic lands she likes to fly
Look up and watch her, way up high!

Value
Totals _____

COLLECTOR'S
VALUE GUIDE™

96

Manny™

Manatee · #4081
Issued: January 7, 1996
Retired: May 11, 1997

Market Value:
④ - $175
③ - $245

Manny is sometimes called a sea cow
She likes to twirl and likes to bow
Manny sure is glad you bought her
Because it's so lonely under water!

Birthdate: June 8, 1995
Price Paid: $_____
Date Purchased: _____
Tag Generation: _____

97

Maple™

(exclusive to Canada)

Bear · #4600
Issued: January 1, 1997
Current – Impossible To Find

Market Value
(in U.S. market):
A. "Maple™" Tush Tag
(Est. Early 97-Current)
⑤ - $240
④ - $260
B. "Pride™" Tush Tag
(Est. Early 97)
④ - $625

B

The
Beanie Babies
Collection™

Pride

HAND MADE IN CHINA
© 1996 TY INC.
OAKBROOK IL U.S.A
SURFACE WASHABLE
ALL NEW MATERIAL
POLYESTER FIBER
& PVC PELLETS CE
REG NO PA 1965KR1

A

Maple the bear likes to ski
With his friends, he plays hockey
He loves his pancakes and eats every crumb
Can you guess which country he's from?

(Canadin money $165.00)

Birthdate: July 1, 1996
Price Paid: $ 80.00
Date Purchased: March 1999
Tag Generation: 5

Mel™

Koala · #4162
Issued: January 1, 1997
Current – Easy To Find
Retired March 31, 1999
Market Value:
5 – $_____
4 – $14

Birthdate: January 15, 1996
Price Paid: $ gift
Date Purchased: Feb. 14, 1999
Tag Generation: 5

How do you name a Koala bear?
It's rather tough, I do declare!
It confuses me, I get into a funk
I'll name him Mel, after my favorite hunk!

99

NEW!

Millenium™

Bear · #4226
Issued: January 1, 1999
Current – Just Released

Market Value:
5 – $_____

Birthdate: January 1, 1999
Price Paid: $ 18:00
Date Purchased: 4-10-99
Tag Generation: 5

A brand new century has come to call
Health and happiness to one and all
Bring on the fireworks and all the fun
Let's keep the party going 'til 2001!

Value
Totals _____

COLLECTOR'S
VALUE GUIDE™

Mooch™

100

NEW!

Spider Monkey · #4224
Issued: January 1, 1999
Current – Just Released

Market Value:
⑤-$_____

Look in the treetops, up towards the sky
Swinging from branches way up high
Tempt him with a banana or fruit
When he's hungry, he acts so cute!

Birthdate: August 1, 1998
Price Paid: $ 5.99
Date Purchased: Feb. 14, 1999
Tag Generation: 5

Mystic™

101

B

Unicorn · #4007
Issued: June 25, 1994
Current – Very Hard To Find

Market Value:
A. Iridescent Horn/Fluffy
   Mane (Dec. 98-Current)
   ⑤-$_____
B. Iridescent Horn/Coarse
   Mane (Oct. 97-Dec. 98)
   ⑤-$10 ④-$23
C. Brown Horn/Coarse Mane
   (Est. Late 95–Oct. 97)
   ④-$42 ③-$120
D. Brown Horn/Fine Mane
   (Est. June 94–Late 95)
   ③-$290 ②-$425 ①-$550

A

C

D

Birthdate: May 21, 1994
Price Paid: $ 5.50
Date Purchased: Feb. 20, 1999
Tag Generation: 5

Once upon a time so far away
A unicorn was born one day in May
Keep Mystic with you, she's a prize
You'll see the magic in her blue eyes!

Value
Totals _____

102

Nana™
(name changed to "Bongo™")

Monkey · #4067
Issued: June 3, 1995
Retired: 1995

Market Value:
❸- $4,050

Birthdate: N/A
Price Paid: $_____
Date Purchased: _____
Tag Generation: _____

No Poem_____
_____
_____
_____

103

Nanook™

Husky · #4104
Issued: May 11, 1997
Current – Easy To Find
Retired march 31, 1999
Market Value:
❺- $_____
❹- $15

Birthdate: November 21, 1996
Price Paid: $ _5.99_
Date Purchased: _Jan. 16, 1999_
Tag Generation: _5_

Nanook is a dog that loves cold weather
To him a sled is light as a feather
Over the snow and through the slush
He runs at hearing the cry of "mush"!

Value
Totals _____

COLLECTOR'S
VALUE GUIDE™

Nibbler™

104
NEW!

Bunny · #4216
Issued: January 1, 1999
Current – Just Released

Market Value:
💗- $_____

Twitching her nose, she looks so sweet
  Small in size, she's very petite
  Soft and furry, hopping with grace
    She'll visit your garden, her favorite place!

Birthdate: April 6, 1998
Price Paid: $ *5.99*
Date Purchased: *Jan. 15, 1999*
Tag Generation: *5*

Nibbly™

105
NEW!

Bunny · #4217
Issued: January 1, 1999
Current – Just Released

Market Value:
💗- $_____

Wonderful ways to spend a day
  Bright and sunny in the month of May
  Hopping around as trees sway
  Looking for friends, out to play!

Birthdate: May 7, 1998
Price Paid: $ *9.25*
Date Purchased: *4-10-99*
Tag Generation: *5*

COLLECTOR'S
VALUE GUIDE™

Value
Totals _____

106

B

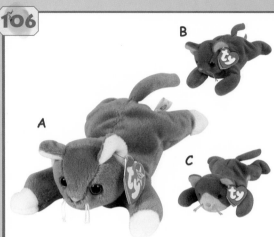

Nip™

Cat • #4003
Issued: January 7, 1995
Retired: December 31, 1997

Market Value:

A. **White Paws**
   (Feb. 96-Dec. 97)
   ⑤-$30 ④-$30 ③-$330
B. **All Gold**
   (Jan. 96–March 96)
   ③-$950
C. **White Face**
   (Jan. 95–Jan. 96)
   ③-$560 ②-$585

A

C

Birthdate: March 6, 1994
Price Paid: $_____
Date Purchased: _____
Tag Generation: _____

His name is Nipper, but we call him Nip
His best friend is a black cat named Zip
Nip likes to run in races for fun
He runs so fast he's always number one!

107

Nuts™

Squirrel • #4114
Issued: January 1, 1997
Retired: January 1, 1999

Market Value:
⑤-$10
④-$13

Birthdate: January 21, 1996
Price Paid: $_5.00_
Date Purchased: _Oct. 1998_
Tag Generation: _5_

With his bushy tail, he'll scamper up a tree
The most cheerful critter you'll ever see,
He's nuts about nuts, and he loves to chat
Have you ever seen a squirrel like that?

Value
Totals _____

COLLECTOR'S
VALUE GUIDE™

Patti™

108

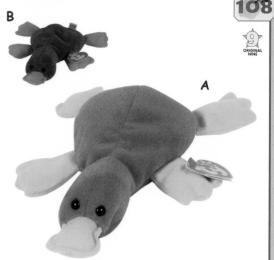

B

A

Platypus · #4025
Issued: January 8, 1994
Retired: May 1, 1998

Market Value:

A. Magenta (Feb. 95-May 98)
⑤- $26
④- $30
③- $250

B. Maroon (Jan. 94–Feb. 95)
③- $825
②- $950
①- $1,030

Ran into Patti one day while walking
Believe me she wouldn't stop talking
Listened and listened to her speak
That would explain her extra large beak!

Birthdate: January 6, 1993
Price Paid: $_____
Date Purchased: _____
Tag Generation: _____

Peace™

109

Bear · #4053
Issued: May 11, 1997
Current – Hard To Find

Market Value:
⑤- $_____
④- $40

All races, all colors, under the sun
Join hands together and have some fun
Dance to the music, rock and roll is the sound
Symbols of peace and love abound!

Birthdate: February 1, 1996
Price Paid: $ 20.00
Date Purchased: Dec. 26, 1998
Tag Generation: 5

110

B

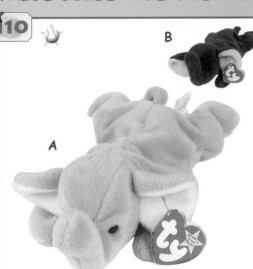

A

Peanut™

Elephant · #4062
Issued: June 3, 1995
Retired: May 1, 1998

Market Value:
A. **Light Blue**
   (Oct. 95-May 98)
   ⑤- $23
   ④- $26
   ③- $1,050
B. **Dark Blue**
   (June 95-Oct. 95)
   ③- $5,000

Birthdate: January 25, 1995
Price Paid: $_____
Date Purchased: _____
Tag Generation: ___5___

Peanut the elephant walks on tip-toes
Quietly sneaking wherever she goes
She'll sneak up on you and a hug
You will get
Peanut is a friend you won't soon forget!

111

Peking™

Panda · #4013
Issued: June 25, 1994
Retired: January 7, 1996

Market Value:
③- $2,150
②- $2,250
①- $2,350

Birthdate: N/A
Price Paid: $_____
Date Purchased: _____
Tag Generation: _____

No Poem _____
_____
_____
_____

Value
Totals _____

112

Pinchers™

Lobster · #4026
Issued: January 8, 1994
Retired: May 1, 1998

Market Value:
A. "Pinchers™" Swing Tag
(Jan. 94-May 98)
⑤-$24
④-$27
③-$110
②-$245
①-$350
B. "Punchers™" Swing Tag
(Est. Early 94)
①-$3,600

B

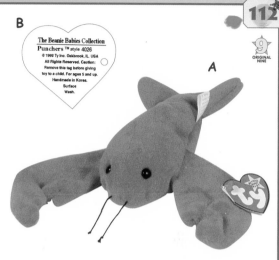

The Beanie Babies Collection
Punchers™ style 4026
© 1993 Ty Inc. Oakbrook, IL USA
All Rights Reserved. Caution:
Remove this tag before giving
toy to a child. For ages 5 and up.
Handmade in Korea.
Surface
Wash.

A

ORIGINAL
NINE

This lobster loves to pinch
    Eating his food inch by inch
        Balancing carefully with his tail
            Moving forward slow as a snail!

Birthdate: June 19, 1993
Price Paid: $_____
Date Purchased: _____
Tag Generation: _____

113

Pinky™

Flamingo · #4072
Issued: June 3, 1995
Retired: January 1, 1999

Market Value:
⑤-$11
④-$14
③-$140

Pinky loves the everglades
    From the hottest pink she's made
        With floppy legs and big orange beak
            She's the Beanie that you seek!

Birthdate: February 13, 1995
Price Paid: $ 5.95
Date Purchased: Jan. 11, 1999
Tag Generation: 5

Value
Totals _____

114 6

Pouch™

Kangaroo · #4161
Issued: January 1, 1997
Current – Easy To Find
Retired March 31, 1999
Market Value:
5- $_____
4- $13

Birthdate: November 6, 1996
Price Paid: $ 5.00
Date Purchased: Feb. 6, 1999
Tag Generation: 4

My little pouch is handy I've found
It helps me carry my baby around
I hop up and down without any fear
Knowing my baby is safe and near.

115

Pounce™

Cat · #4122
Issued: December 31, 1997
Current – Easy To Find
Retired March 31, 1999
Market Value:
5- $_____

Birthdate: August 28, 1997
Price Paid: $_____
Date Purchased: _____
Tag Generation: _____

Sneaking and slinking down the hall
To pounce upon a fluffy yarn ball
Under the tables, around the chairs
Through the rooms and down the stairs!

Value
Totals _____

COLLECTOR'S
VALUE GUIDE™

116

Prance™

Cat · #4123
Issued: December 31, 1997
Current – Easy To Find
Retired March 31, 1999
Market Value:
⑤- $_____

She darts around and swats the air
   Then looks confused when nothing's there
   Pick her up and pet her soft fur
   Listen closely, and you'll hear her purr!

Birthdate: November 20, 1997
Price Paid: $_____
Date Purchased: _____
Tag Generation: _____5_____

117

NEW!

Prickles™

Hedgehog · #4220
Issued: January 1, 1999
Current – Just Released

Market Value:
⑤- $_____

Prickles the hedgehog loves to play
   She rolls around the meadow all day
   Tucking under her feet and head
   Suddenly she looks like a ball instead!

Birthdate: February 19, 1998
Price Paid: $ *5.99*
Date Purchased: *Jan. 13, 1999*
Tag Generation: _____5_____

Value
Totals _____

118

B

The
Beanie Babies
Collection.®

★ ty ™

Princess™

HANDMADE IN CHINA
© 1997 TY INC.
OAKBROOK, IL. U.S.A.
SURFACE WASHABLE
ALL NEW MATERIAL
POLYESTER FIBER
& P.V.C. PELLETS CE
REG. NO. PA. 1965(KR)

A

Princess™

Bear · #4300
Issued: October 29, 1997
Current - Hard To Find
Retired april 13, 1999
Market Value:
A. "P.E. Pellets" On Tush Tag
(Est. Late 97-Current)
④- $_____
B. "P.V.C. Pellets" On Tush
Tag (Est. Late 97)
④- $145

Birthdate: N/A
Price Paid: $ *gift (5.00)*
Date Purchased: *nov. 1998*
Tag Generation: *4*

Like an angel, she came from heaven above
She shared her compassion, her pain, her love
She only stayed with us long enough to teach
The world to share, to give, to reach.

119

Puffer™

Puffin · #4181
Issued: December 31, 1997
Retired: September 18, 1998

Market Value:
⑤- $13

Birthdate: November 3, 1997
Price Paid: $ *5.99*
Date Purchased: *Jan. 4, 1999*
Tag Generation: *5*

What in the world does a puffin do?
We're sure that you would like to know too
We asked Puffer how she spends her days
Before she answered, she flew away!

Value
Totals _____

COLLECTOR'S
VALUE GUIDE™

120

Pugsly™

Pug Dog · #4106
Issued: May 11, 1997
Current - Easy To Find
Retired March 31, 1999
Market Value:
5- $_____
4- $14

Pugsly is picky about what he will wear
Never a spot, a stain or a tear
Image is something of which he'll gloat
Until he noticed his wrinkled coat!

Birthdate: May 2, 1996
Price Paid: $ 5.00
Date Purchased: *Jan. 9, 1999*
Tag Generation: 5

121

Pumkin™

Pumpkin · #4205
Issued: September 30, 1998
Retired: January 1, 1999

Market Value:
5- $35

Ghost and goblins are out tonight
Witches try hard to cause fright
This little pumpkin is very sweet
He only wants to trick or treat!

Birthdate: October 31, 1998
Price Paid: $ 5.00
Date Purchased: *Feb. 5, 1999*
Tag Generation: 5

122

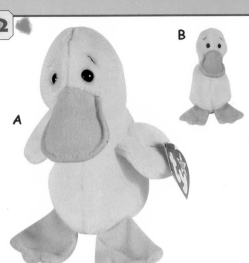

B

Quackers™

Duck · #4024
Issued: June 25, 1994
Retired: May 1, 1998

Market Value:
A. "Quackers™" With Wings
(Jan. 95–May 98)
⑤-$22 ④-$25
❸-$115 ❷-$825
B. "Quacker™" Without
Wings (June 94–Jan. 95)
❷-$2,100 ❶-$2,300

A

Birthdate: April 19, 1994
Price Paid: $ 12.00
Date Purchased: April 9, 1999
Tag Generation: 4

There is a duck by the name of Quackers
Every night he eats animal crackers
He swims in a lake that's clear and blue
But he'll come to the shore to be with you!

123

Radar™

Bat · #4091
Issued: September 1, 1995
Retired: May 11, 1997

Market Value:
④-$185
❸-$255

Birthdate: October 30, 1995
Price Paid: $_____
Date Purchased: _____
Tag Generation: _____

Radar the bat flies late at night
He can soar to an amazing height
If you see something as high as a star
Take a good look, it might be Radar!

Value
Totals _____

COLLECTOR'S
VALUE GUIDE™

124

Rainbow™

B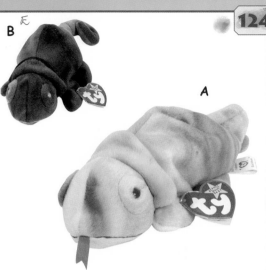

Chameleon · #4037
Issued: December 31, 1997
Current – Easy To Find
Retired March 31, 1999
Market Value:

A. Tie-dye/With Tongue
   (Mid 98-Current)
   ⑤- $_____

B. Blue/No Tongue
   (Dec. 97-Mid 98)
   ⑤- $12

A

Red, green, blue and yellow
  This chameleon is a colorful fellow.
  A blend of colors, his own unique hue
  Rainbow was made especially for you!

Birthdate: October 14, 1997
Price Paid: $ *5.99*
Date Purchased: *Jan. 6, 1999*
Tag Generation: *5*
Me & E.

125

Rex™

Tyrannosaurus · #4086
Issued: June 3, 1995
Retired: June 15, 1996

Market Value:
  ③- $925

No Poem_____
_____
_____
_____

Birthdate: N/A
Price Paid: $_____
Date Purchased: _____
Tag Generation: _____

126

Righty™

Elephant · #4086
Issued: June 15, 1996
Retired: January 1, 1997

Market Value:
❹- $300

Birthdate: July 4, 1996
Price Paid: $_____
Date Purchased: _____
Tag Generation: _____

Donkeys to the left, elephants to the right
Often seems like a crazy sight
This whole game seems very funny
Until you realize they're spending
Your money!

127

Ringo™

Raccoon · #4014
Issued: January 7, 1996
Retired: September 16, 1998

Market Value:
❺- $13
❹- $16
❸- $92

Birthdate: July 14, 1995
Price Paid: $_____
Date Purchased: _____
Tag Generation: _____

Ringo hides behind his mask
He will come out, if you should ask
He loves to chitter. He loves to chatter
Just about anything, it doesn't matter!

Value
Totals _____

COLLECTOR'S
VALUE GUIDE™

128

Roam™

Buffalo · #4209
Issued: September 30, 1998
Current – Moderate To Find

Market Value:
⑤- $_____

Once roaming wild on American land
Tall and strong, wooly and grand
So rare and special is this guy
Find him quickly, he's quite a buy!

Birthdate: September 27, 1998
Price Paid: $ 5.50
Date Purchased: Jan. 15, 1999
Tag Generation: 5

129

Roary™

Lion · #4069
Issued: May 11, 1997
Retired: January 1, 1999

Market Value:
⑤- $12
④- $15

Deep in the jungle they crowned him king
But being brave is not his thing
A cowardly lion some may say
He hears his roar and runs away!

Birthdate: February 20, 1996
Price Paid: $ 5.50
Date Purchased: Feb. 2, 1999
Tag Generation: 5

Value
Totals _____

130

Rocket™

Blue Jay · #4202
Issued: May 30, 1998
Current – Easy To Find

Market Value:
⑤- $_____

Birthdate: March 12, 1997
Price Paid: $ 5.99
Date Purchased: Dec. 26, 1998
Tag Generation: 5

Rocket is the fastest blue jay ever
He flies in all sorts of weather
Aerial tricks are his specialty
He's so entertaining for you and me!

131

Rover™

Dog · #4101
Issued: June 15, 1996
Retired: May 1, 1998

Market Value:
⑤- $23
④- $27

Birthdate: May 30, 1996
Price Paid: $ trade ($30.00)
Date Purchased: Jan. 25, 1999
Tag Generation: 4

This dog is red and his name is Rover
If you call him he is sure to come over
He barks and plays with all his might
But worry not, he won't bite!

Value
Totals _____

COLLECTOR'S
VALUE GUIDE™

Sammy™

132

NEW!

Bear · #4215
Issued: January 1, 1999
Current – Just Released

Market Value:
🌀- $_____

As Sammy steps up to the plate
The crowd gets excited, can hardly wait
We know Sammy won't let us down
He makes us the happiest fans in town!

Birthdate: June 23, 1998
Price Paid: $ *5.99*
Date Purchased: *Feb 18, 1999*
Tag Generation: *5*

Santa™

133

Elf · #4203
Issued: September 30, 1998
Retired: January 1, 1999

Market Value:
🌀-$38

Known by all in his suit of red
Piles of presents on his sled
Generous and giving, he brings us joy
Peace and love, plus this special toy!

Birthdate: December 6, 1998
Price Paid: $_____
Date Purchased: _____
Tag Generation: _____

COLLECTOR'S
VALUE GUIDE™

Value
Totals _____

138

Seamore™

Seal · #4029
Issued: June 25, 1994
Retired: October 1, 1997

Market Value:
- ❹ - $165
- ❸ - $240
- ❷ - $370
- ❶ - $520

Birthdate: December 14, 1996
Price Paid: $_____
Date Purchased: _____
Tag Generation: _____

Seamore is a little white seal
Fish and clams are her favorite meal
Playing and laughing in the sand
She's the happiest seal in the land!

139

Seaweed™

Otter · #4080
Issued: January 7, 1996
Retired: September 19, 1998

Market Value:
- ❺ - $28
- ❹ - $32
- ❸ - $105

Birthdate: March 19, 1996
Price Paid: $ _5.00_
Date Purchased: _may   1998_
Tag Generation: _5_
                _E._

Seaweed is what she likes to eat
It's supposed to be a delicious treat
Have you tried a treat from the water
If you haven't, maybe you "otter"!

Value
Totals _____

COLLECTOR'S
VALUE GUIDE™

140 NEW!

Slippery™

Seal · #4222
Issued: January 1, 1999
Current – Just Released

Market Value:
❺-$_____

In the ocean, near a breaking wave
Slippery the seal acts very brave
On his surfboard, he sees a swell
He's riding the wave! Oooops...he fell!

Birthdate: January 17, 1998
Price Paid: $ *5.50*
Date Purchased: *Feb. 8, 1999*
Tag Generation: *5*

141

Slither™

Snake · #4031
Issued: June 25, 1994
Retired: June 15, 1995

Market Value:
❸-$2,050
❷-$2,100
❶-$2,300

No Poem_____
_____
_____
_____

Birthdate: N/A
Price Paid: $_____
Date Purchased: _____
Tag Generation: _____

142

B

A

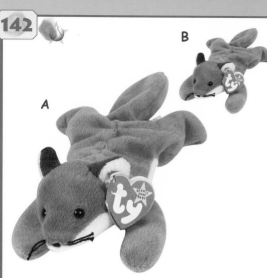

Sly™

Fox · #4115
Issued: June 15, 1996
Retired: September 22, 1998

Market Value:
A. White Belly
(Aug. 96-Sept. 98)
⑤ - $13
④ - $16
B. Brown Belly
(June 96-Aug. 96)
④ - $180

Birthdate: September 12, 1996
Price Paid: $ 7.99
Date Purchased: Feb. 4, 1999
Tag Generation: 4

Sly is a fox and tricky is he
Please don't chase him, let him be
If you want him, just say when
He'll peek out from his den!

143

Smoochy™

Frog · #4039
Issued: December 31, 1997
Current - Easy To Find
Retired march 31, 1999
Market Value:
⑤ - $_____

Birthdate: October 1, 1997
Price Paid: $ 5.00
Date Purchased: Sept. 1998
Tag Generation: 5
E. 4D #4.00 4-8-99

Is he a frog or maybe a prince?
This confusion makes him wince
Find the answer, help him with this
Be the one to give him a kiss!

Value
Totals _____

COLLECTOR'S
VALUE GUIDE™

144

Snip™

Siamese Cat · #4120
Issued: January 1, 1997
Retired: January 1, 1999

Market Value:
- ❤5- $11
- ❤4- $14

Snip the cat is Siamese
She'll be your friend if you please
So toss her a toy or a piece of string
    Playing with you is her favorite thing!

Birthdate: October 22, 1996
Price Paid: $_____
Date Purchased: _____
Tag Generation: _____

145

Snort™

Bull · #4002
Issued: January 1, 1997
Retired: September 15, 1998

Market Value:
- ❤5- $13
- ❤4- $16

Although Snort is not so tall
He loves to play basketball
He is a star player in his dreams
Can you guess his favorite team?

Birthdate: May 15, 1995
Price Paid: $_5.00_
Date Purchased: _June_ _1998_
Tag Generation: _5_
    _Ed_

146

Snowball™

Snowman · #4201
Issued: October 1, 1997
Retired: December 31, 1997

Market Value:
❹ - $48

Birthdate: December 22, 1996
Price Paid: $_____
Date Purchased: _____
Tag Generation: _____

There is a snowman, I've been told
That plays with Beanies out in the cold
What is better in a winter wonderland
Than a Beanie snowman in your hand!

147

Sparky™

Dalmatian · #4100
Issued: June 15, 1996
Retired: May 11, 1997

Market Value:
❹ - $155

Birthdate: February 27, 1996
Price Paid: $_____
Date Purchased: _____
Tag Generation: _____

Sparky rides proud on the fire truck
Ringing the bell and pushing his luck
He gets under foot when trying to help
He often gets stepped on and
Lets out a yelp!

Value
Totals _____

COLLECTOR'S
VALUE GUIDE™

148

Speedy™

Turtle • #4030
Issued: June 25, 1994
Retired: October 1, 1997

Market Value:
4 – $38
3 – $125
2 – $240
1 – $360

Speedy ran marathons in the past
Such a shame, always last
Now Speedy is a big star
After he bought a racing car!

Birthdate: August 14, 1994
Price Paid: $ _16.66_
Date Purchased: _Feb. 13, 1999_
Tag Generation: _____
_E._

149

Spike™

Rhinoceros • #4060
Issued: June 15, 1996
Retired: January 1, 1999

Market Value:
5 – $11
4 – $15

Spike the rhino likes to stampede
He's the bruiser that you need
Gentle to birds on his back and spike
You can be his friend if you like!

Birthdate: August 13, 1996
Price Paid: $ _5.99_
Date Purchased: _Dec. 15, 1998_
Tag Generation: _5_
_E._

150

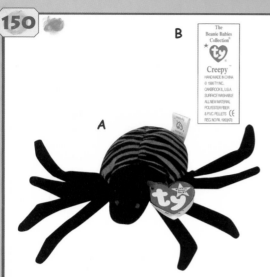

B

The
Beanie Babies
Collection®
★ ty
Creepy
HANDMADE IN CHINA
© 1996 TY INC.
OAKBROOK, IL U.S.A.
SURFACE WASHABLE
ALL NEW MATERIAL
POLYESTER FIBER
& PVC PELLETS CE
REG. NO. PA. 1965 (KY)

A

Spinner™

Spider · #4036
Issued: October 1, 1997
Retired: September 19, 1998

Market Value:
A. "Spinner™" Tush Tag
(Oct. 97–Sept. 98)
⑤– $12
④– $17
B. "Creepy™" Tush Tag
(Est. Late 97–Sept. 98)
⑤– $45

Birthdate: October 28, 1996
Price Paid: $ 5.99
Date Purchased: Dec. 15, 1998
Tag Generation: 5
E.

Does this spider make you scared?
Among many people that feeling is shared
Remember spiders have feelings too
In fact, this spider really likes you!

151

9
ORIGINAL
NINE

Splash™

Whale · #4022
Issued: January 8, 1994
Retired: May 11, 1997

Market Value:
④– $130
③– $215
②– $370
①– $550

Birthdate: July 8, 1993
Price Paid: $_____
Date Purchased: _____
Tag Generation: _____

Splash loves to jump and dive
He's the fastest whale alive
He always wins the 100 yard dash
With a victory jump he'll make a splash!

Value
Totals _____

COLLECTOR'S
VALUE GUIDE™

152

Spooky™

B

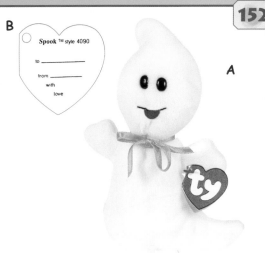

Spook ™ style 4090

to _____

from _____

with

love

A

Ghost · #4090
Issued: September 1, 1995
Retired: December 31, 1997

Market Value:
A. "Spooky™" Swing Tag
(Est. Late 95-Dec. 97)
④-$44
③-$155
B. "Spook™" Swing Tag
(Est. Sept. 95-Late 95)
③-$450

Ghosts can be a scary sight
But don't let Spooky bring you any fright
Because when you're alone, you will see
The best friend that Spooky can be!

Birthdate: October 31, 1995
Price Paid: $_____
Date Purchased: _____
Tag Generation: _____

153

Spot™

B

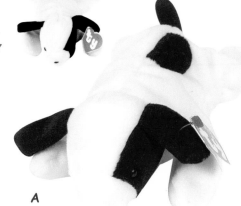

9
ORIGINAL
NINE

A

Dog · #4000
Issued: January 8, 1994
Retired: October 1, 1997

Market Value:
A. With Spot
(April 94-Oct. 97)
④-$58
③-$145
②-$825
B. Without Spot
(Jan. 94–April 94)
②-$2,000
①-$2,200

See Spot sprint, see Spot run
You and Spot will have lots of fun
Watch out now, because he's not slow
Just stand back and watch him go!

Birthdate: January 3, 1993
Price Paid: $_____
Date Purchased: _____
Tag Generation: _____

Value
Totals _____

154

Spunky™

Cocker Spaniel • #4184
Issued: December 31, 1997
Current – Easy To Find
Retired March 31, 1999
Market Value:
⑤ – $_____

Birthdate: January 14, 1997
Price Paid: $ *5.00*
Date Purchased: *June , 1998*
Tag Generation: *5*
Ed

Bouncing around without much grace
To jump on your lap and lick your face
But watch him closely he has no fears
He'll run so fast he'll trip over his ears

155

ORIGINAL NINE

Squealer™

Pig • #4005
Issued: January 8, 1994
Retired: May 1, 1998

Market Value:
⑤ – $33
④ – $36
③ – $115
② – $260
① – $370

Birthdate: April 23, 1993
Price Paid: $_____
Date Purchased: _____
Tag Generation: _____

Squealer likes to joke around
He is known as class clown
Listen to his stories awhile
There is no doubt he'll make you smile!

Value
Totals _____

COLLECTOR'S
VALUE GUIDE™

156

Steg™

Stegosaurus · #4087
Issued: June 3, 1995
Retired: June 15, 1996

Market Value:
 – $1,000

No Poem_____
_____
_____
_____

Birthdate: N/A
Price Paid: $_____
Date Purchased: _____
Tag Generation: _____

157

Stilts™

NEW!

Stork · #4221
Issued: January 1, 1999
Current – Just Released

Market Value:
 – $_____

Flying high over mountains and streams
Fulfilling wishes, hopes and dreams
The stork brings parents bundles of joy
The greatest gift, a girl or boy!

Birthdate: June 16, 1998
Price Paid: $ 5.99
Date Purchased: Jan. 15, 1999
Tag Generation: 5

158

Sting™

Stingray · #4077
Issued: June 3, 1995
Retired: January 1, 1997

Market Value:
❹- $195
❸- $275

Birthdate: August 27, 1995
Price Paid: $_____
Date Purchased: _____
Tag Generation: _____

I'm a manta ray and my name is Sting
I'm quite unusual and this is the thing
Under the water I glide like a bird
Have you ever seen something so absurd?

159

Stinger™

Scorpion · #4193
Issued: May 30, 1998
Retired: January 1, 1999

Market Value:
❺- $15

Birthdate: September 29, 1997
Price Paid: $ 4.99
Date Purchased: Dec. 15, 1998
Tag Generation: 5
E.

Stinger the scorpion will run and dart
But this little fellow is really all heart
So if you see him don't run away
Say hello and ask him to play!

Value Totals _____

COLLECTOR'S
VALUE GUIDE™

160

Stinky™

Skunk · #4017
Issued: June 3, 1995
Retired: September 28, 1998

Market Value:
- ⑤-$16
- ④-$19
- ③-$95

Deep in the woods he lived in a cave
Perfume and mints were the gifts he gave
He showered every night in the kitchen sink
Hoping one day he wouldn't stink!

Birthdate: February 13, 1995
Price Paid: $ 5.00
Date Purchased: June 26, 1999
Tag Generation: 5

161

Stretch™

Ostrich · #4182
Issued: December 31, 1997
Current – Easy To Find
Retired March 31, 1999
Market Value:
- ⑤-$_____

She thinks when her head is underground
The rest of her body can't be found
The Beanie Babies think it's absurd
To play hide and seek with this bird!

Birthdate: September 21, 1997
Price Paid: $ free (5.95)
Date Purchased: Jan. 15, 1999
Tag Generation: 5

Value
Totals _____

162

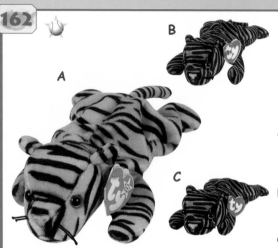

B

A

C

Stripes™

Tiger · #4065
Issued: Est. June 3, 1995
Retired: May 1, 1998

Market Value:
**A. Light w/Fewer Stripes
(June 96-May 98)**
⑤- $20
④- $24
**B. Dark w/Fuzzy Belly
(Est. Early 96-June 96)**
③- $1,100
**C. Dark w/More Stripes
(Est. June 95-Early 96)**
③- $400

Birthdate: June 11, 1995
Price Paid: $_____
Date Purchased: _____
Tag Generation: _____

*Stripes was never fierce nor strong
So with tigers, he didn't get along
Jungle life was hard to get by
So he came to his friends at Ty!*

163

Strut™
(name changed from "Doodle™")

Rooster · #4171
Issued: July 12, 1997
Current - Easy To Find
Retired march 31, 199
Market Value:
⑤- $_____
④- $18

Birthdate: March 8, 1996
Price Paid: $_____
Date Purchased: _____
Tag Generation: _____

*Listen closely to "cock-a-doodle-doo"
What's the rooster saying to you?
Hurry, wake up sleepy head
We have lots to do, get out of bed!*

Value
Totals _____

COLLECTOR'S
VALUE GUIDE™

164

Tabasco™

Bull · #4002
Issued: June 3, 1995
Retired: January 1, 1997

Market Value:
④–$200
③–$275

Although Tabasco is not so tall
He loves to play basketball
He is a star player in his dream
Can you guess his favorite team?

Birthdate: May 15, 1995
Price Paid: $_____
Date Purchased: _____
Tag Generation: _____

165

Tank™

B

Armadillo · #4031
Issued: Est. January 7, 1996
Retired: October 1, 1997

A

Market Value:
A. 9 Plates/With Shell
(Est. Late 96-Oct. 97)
④–$85
B. 9 Plates/Without Shell
(Est. Mid 96-Late 96)
④–$240
C. 7 Plates/Without Shell
(Est. Jan. 96-Mid 96)
③–$225

C

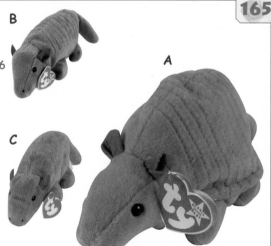

This armadillo lives in the South
Shoving Tex-Mex in his mouth
He sure loves it south of the border
Keeping his friends in good order!

Birthdate: February 22, 1995
Price Paid: $_____
Date Purchased: _____
Tag Generation: _____

Value
Totals _____

166

A

B

Teddy™ (brown)

Bear • #4050
Issued: June 25, 1994
Retired: October 1, 1997

Market Value:
A. New Face (Jan. 95-Oct. 97)
④- $105
③- $390
②- $1,000
B. Old Face (June 94-Jan. 95)
②- $2,800
①- $3,000

Birthdate: November 28, 1995
Price Paid: $_____
Date Purchased: _____
Tag Generation: _____

Teddy wanted to go out today
All of his friends went out to play
But he'd rather help whatever you do
After all, his best friend is you!

167

A

B

Teddy™ (cranberry)

Bear • #4052
Issued: June 25, 1994
Retired: January 7, 1996

Market Value:
A. New Face (Jan. 95-Jan. 96)
③- $1,900
②- $2,000
B. Old Face (June 94-Jan. 95)
②- $1,800
①- $1,900

Birthdate: N/A
Price Paid: $_____
Date Purchased: _____
Tag Generation: _____

No Poem_____
_____
_____
_____

Value
Totals _____

COLLECTOR'S
VALUE GUIDE™

168

Teddy™ (jade)

Bear · #4057
Issued: June 25, 1994
Retired: January 7, 1996

Market Value:
A. New Face (Jan. 95-Jan. 96)
  ❸- $1,900
  ❷- $2,000
B. Old Face (June 94-Jan. 95)
  ❷- $1,800
  ❶- $1,900

No Poem_____
_____
_____
_____

Birthdate: N/A
Price Paid: $_____
Date Purchased: _____
Tag Generation: _____

169

Teddy™ (magenta)

Bear · #4056
Issued: June 25, 1994
Retired: January 7, 1996

Market Value:
A. New Face (Jan. 95-Jan. 96)
  ❸- $1,900
  ❷- $2,000
B. Old Face (June 94-Jan. 95)
  ❷- $1,800
  ❶- $1,900

No Poem_____
_____
_____
_____

Birthdate: N/A
Price Paid: $_____
Date Purchased: _____
Tag Generation: _____

170

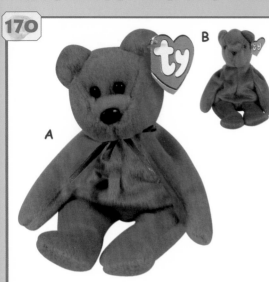

A

B

Teddy™ (teal)

Bear · #4051
Issued: June 25, 1994
Retired: January 7, 1996

Market Value:
A. New Face (Jan. 95-Jan. 96)
❸- $1,900
❷- $2,000
B. Old Face (June 94-Jan. 95)
❷- $1,800
❶- $1,900

Birthdate: N/A
Price Paid: $_____
Date Purchased: _____
Tag Generation: _____

No Poem_____
_____
_____
_____

171

A

B

C

Teddy™ (violet)

Bear · #4055
Issued: June 25, 1994
Retired: January 7, 1996

Market Value:
A. New Face (Jan. 95-Jan. 96)
❸- $1,900
❷- $2,000
B. New Face/Employee Bear
w/Red Tush Tag
(Green or Red Ribbon)
No Swing Tag – $4,000
C. Old Face (June 94-Jan. 95)
❷- $1,800
❶- $1,900

Birthdate: N/A
Price Paid: $_____
Date Purchased: _____
Tag Generation: _____

No Poem_____
_____
_____
_____

Value
Totals _____

COLLECTOR'S
VALUE GUIDE™

Tiny™

172

NEW!

Chihuahua · #4234
Issued: January 1, 1999
Current – Just Released

Market Value:
⑤- $_____

South of the Border, in the sun
Tiny the Chihuahua is having fun
Attending fiestas, breaking piñatas
Eating a taco, or some enchiladas!

Birthdate: September 8, 1998
Price Paid: $ 5.99
Date Purchased: Jan. 11, 1999
Tag Generation: _____

Tracker™

173

Basset Hound · #4198
Issued: May 30, 1998
Current – Easy To Find

Market Value:
⑤- $_____

Sniffing and tracking and following trails
Tracker the basset always wags his tail
It doesn't matter what you do
He's always happy when he's with you!

Birthdate: June 5, 1997
Price Paid: $ 5.99
Date Purchased: Dec. 26 1998
Tag Generation: 5

174

Trap™

Mouse · #4042
Issued: June 25, 1994
Retired: June 15, 1995

Market Value:
❸ - $1,600
❷ - $1,700
❶ - $1,850

Birthdate: N/A
Price Paid: $_____
Date Purchased: _____
Tag Generation: _____

No Poem _____
_____
_____
_____

175

Tuffy™

Terrier · #4108
Issued: May 11, 1997
Retired: January 1, 1999

Market Value:
❺ - $12
❹ - $16

Birthdate: October 12, 1996
Price Paid: $ 4.99
Date Purchased: Dec. 15, 1998
Tag Generation: 5

Taking off with a thunderous blast
Tuffy rides his motorcycle fast
The Beanies roll with laughs and squeals
He never took off his training wheels!

Value
Totals _____

COLLECTOR'S
VALUE GUIDE™

176

Tusk™

Walrus · #4076
Issued: Est. June 3, 1995
Retired: January 1, 1997

Market Value:
A. "Tusk™" Swing Tag
(Est. June 95-Jan. 97)
④- $150
③- $230
B. "Tuck™" Swing Tag
(Est. Early 96-Jan. 97)
④- $175

B

Tuck™ style 4076
DATE OF BIRTH : 9·18·95

Tusk brushes his teeth everyday
To keep them shiny, it's the only way
Teeth are special, so you must try
And they will sparkle when
You say "Hi"!

Visit our web page!!!
http://www.ty.com

A

Tusk brushes his teeth everyday
To keep them shiny, it's the only way
Teeth are special, so you must try
And they will sparkle when
You say "Hi"!

Birthdate: September 18, 1995
Price Paid: $_____
Date Purchased: _____
Tag Generation: _____

177

Twigs™

Giraffe · #4068
Issued: January 7, 1996
Retired: May 1, 1998

Market Value:
⑤- $25
④- $28
③- $115

Twigs has his head in the clouds
He stands tall, he stands proud
With legs so skinny they wobble and shake
What an unusual friend he will make!

Birthdate: May 19, 1995
Price Paid: $ 12100
Date Purchased: June 26 1999
Tag Generation: 5

Value
Totals _____

178

NEW!

Valentina™

Bear · #4233
Issued: January 1, 1999
Current – Just Released

Market Value:
⑤- $_____

Birthdate: February 14, 1998
Price Paid: $ 6.00
Date Purchased: FEB. 14, 1999
Tag Generation: 5

Flowers, candy and hearts galore
Sweet words of love for those you adore
With this bear comes love that's true
On Valentine's Day and all year through!

179

Valentino™

Bear · #4058
Issued: January 7, 1995
Retired: January 1, 1999

Market Value:
⑤- $28
④- $33
③- $155
②- $260

Birthdate: February 14, 1994
Price Paid: $ 13.50
Date Purchased: Dec. 29, 1998
Tag Generation: 5

His heart is red and full of love
He cares for you so give him a hug
Keep him close when feeling blue
Feel the love he has for you!

Value
Totals _____

COLLECTOR'S
VALUE GUIDE™

180

Velvet™

Panther · #4064
Issued: June 3, 1995
Retired: October 1, 1997

Market Value:
④- $40
③- $125

Velvet loves to sleep in the trees
Lulled to dreams by the buzz of the bees
She snoozes all day and plays all night
Running and jumping in the moonlight!

Birthdate: December 16, 1995
Price Paid: $_____
Date Purchased: _____
Tag Generation: _____

181

Waddle™

Penguin · #4075
Issued: June 3, 1995
Retired: May 1, 1998

Market Value:
⑤- $26
④- $30
③- $110

Waddle the Penguin likes to dress up
Every night he wears his tux
When Waddle walks, it never fails
He always trips over his tails!

Birthdate: December 19, 1995
Price Paid: $_____
Date Purchased: _____
Tag Generation: _____

182

Waves™

Whale · #4084
Issued: May 11, 1997
Retired: May 1, 1998

Market Value:
5 - $24
4 - $28

Birthdate: December 8, 1996
Price Paid: $_____
Date Purchased: _____
Tag Generation: _____

Join him today on the Internet
Don't be afraid to get your feet wet
He taught all the Beanies how to surf
Our web page is his home turf!

183

Web™

Spider · #4041
Issued: June 25, 1994
Retired: January 7, 1996

Market Value:
3 - $1,500
2 - $1,600
1 - $1,750

Birthdate: N/A
Price Paid: $_____
Date Purchased: _____
Tag Generation: _____

No Poem_____
_____
_____
_____

Value
Totals _____

COLLECTOR'S
VALUE GUIDE™

184

Weenie™

Dachshund · #4013
Issued: January 7, 1996
Retired: May 1, 1998

Market Value:
- ⑤- $33
- ④- $38
- ③- $122

Weenie the dog is quite a sight
Long of body and short of height
He perches himself high on a log
And considers himself to be top dog!

TOP DOG

Birthdate: July 20, 1995
Price Paid: $ _16,66_
Date Purchased: _Feb. 13, 1998_
Tag Generation: _5_

185

Whisper™

Deer · #4194
Issued: May 30, 1998
Current – Easy To Find

Market Value:
- ⑤- $_____

She's very shy as you can see
When she hides behind a tree
With big brown eyes and soft to touch
This little fawn will love you so much!

Birthdate: April 5, 1997
Price Paid: $ _4.95_
Date Purchased: _Jan. 13, 1999_
Tag Generation: _5_

Value
Totals _____

186

Wise™

Owl · #4187
Issued: May 30, 1998
Retired: January 1, 1999

Market Value:
⑤- $27

Birthdate: May 31, 1997
Price Paid: $ 6.99
Date Purchased: Feb.5,1999
Tag Generation: 5

Wise is at the head of the class
With A's and B's he'll always pass
He's got his diploma and feels really great
Meet the newest graduate: Class of '98!

187

Wrinkles™

Bulldog · #4103
Issued: June 15, 1996
Retired: September 22, 1998

Market Value:
⑤- $16
④- $19

Birthdate: May 1, 1996
Price Paid: $ 5.75
Date Purchased: Jan.18,1999
Tag Generation: 5

This little dog is named Wrinkles
His nose is soft and often crinkles
Likes to climb up on your lap
He's a cheery sort of chap!

Value
Totals _____

COLLECTOR'S
VALUE GUIDE™

188

Zero™

Penguin • #4207
Issued: September 30, 1998
Retired: January 1, 1999

Market Value:
❺-$35

Penguins love the ice and snow
Playing in weather twenty below
Antarctica is where I love to be
Splashing in the cold, cold sea!

Birthdate: January 2, 1998
Price Paid: $ _5.00_
Date Purchased: _Jan. 28, 1999_
Tag Generation: _5_

189

Ziggy™

Zebra • #4063
Issued: June 3, 1995
Retired: May 1, 1998

Market Value:
❺-$26
❹-$30
❸-$110

Ziggy likes soccer – he's a referee
That way he watches the games for free
The other Beanies don't think it's fair
But Ziggy the Zebra doesn't care!

Birthdate: December 24, 1995
Price Paid: $_____
Date Purchased: _____
Tag Generation: _____

Value
Totals _____

190

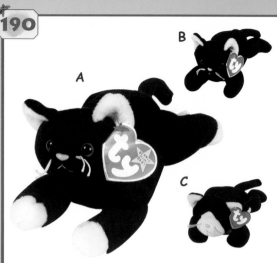

A

B

C

Zip™

Cat · #4004
Issued: January 7, 1995
Retired: May 1, 1998

Market Value:

A. White Paws
(March 96-May 98)
⑤-$45 ④-$50 ③-$550

B. All Black
(Jan. 96-March 96)
③-$1,850

C. White Face
(Jan. 95-Jan. 96)
③-$540 ②-$600

Birthdate: March 28, 1994
Price Paid: $_____
Date Purchased: _____
Tag Generation: _____

Keep Zip by your side all the day through
Zip is good luck, you'll see it's true
When you have something you need to do
Zip will always believe in you!

Welcome To All Of Our New Friends!

Value
Totals _____

COLLECTOR'S
VALUE GUIDE™

BEANIE BABIES® ARE A HIT AT SPORTING EVENTS!

Sports teams across the country have noticed a new breed of fans at their games – the short, furry kind! These cuddly creatures and their commemorative cards, offered as a promotion to increase attendance at games, have become a hit with sports fans and collectors alike. In addition, they have drawn a lot of attention on the secondary market, particularly if they are offered with a ticket stub from the event.

FUTURE PROMOTIONS

Look for new promotions to be announced soon by the Sacramento Kings of the NBA with "Claude" and "Fortune" and the St. Louis Blues of the NHL with an undetermined *Beanie Baby*.

SPORTS PROMOTION BEANIE BABIES® KEY

Canadian Special Olympics	National Basketball Association	National Hockey League
Major League Baseball	National Football League	Women's National Basketball Association

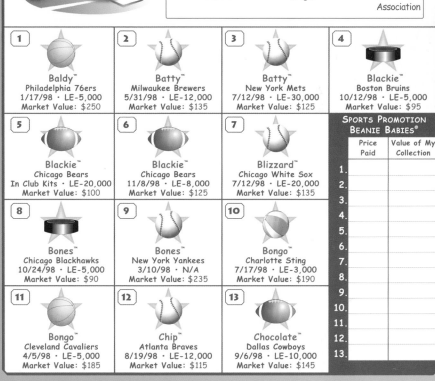

1
Baldy™
Philadelphia 76ers
1/17/98 · LE-5,000
Market Value: $250

2
Batty™
Milwaukee Brewers
5/31/98 · LE-12,000
Market Value: $135

3
Batty™
New York Mets
7/12/98 · LE-30,000
Market Value: $125

4
Blackie™
Boston Bruins
10/12/98 · LE-5,000
Market Value: $95

5
Blackie™
Chicago Bears
In Club Kits · LE-20,000
Market Value: $100

6
Blackie™
Chicago Bears
11/8/98 · LE-8,000
Market Value: $125

7
Blizzard™
Chicago White Sox
7/12/98 · LE-20,000
Market Value: $135

8
Bones™
Chicago Blackhawks
10/24/98 · LE-5,000
Market Value: $90

9
Bones™
New York Yankees
3/10/98 · N/A
Market Value: $235

10
Bongo™
Charlotte Sting
7/17/98 · LE-3,000
Market Value: $190

11
Bongo™
Cleveland Cavaliers
4/5/98 · LE-5,000
Market Value: $185

12
Chip™
Atlanta Braves
8/19/98 · LE-12,000
Market Value: $115

13
Chocolate™
Dallas Cowboys
9/6/98 · LE-10,000
Market Value: $145

SPORTS PROMOTION BEANIE BABIES®

	Price Paid	Value of My Collection
1.		
2.		
3.		
4.		
5.		
6.		
7.		
8.		
9.		
10.		
11.		
12.		
13.		

Value Totals _____

14
Chocolate™
Denver Nuggets
4/17/98 · LE-5,000
Market Value: $185

15
Chocolate™
Seattle Mariners
9/5/98 · LE-10,000
Market Value: $110

16
Chocolate™
Tennessee Oilers
10/18/98 · LE-7,500
Market Value: $115

17
Chocolate™
Toronto Maple Leafs
1/2/99 · LE-3,000
Market Value: N/E

18
Cubbie™
Chicago Cubs
1/16-1/18/98 · LE-100
Market Value: $450

19
Cubbie™
Chicago Cubs
5/18/97 · LE-10,000
Market Value: $215

20
Cubbie™
Chicago Cubs
9/6/97 · LE-10,000
Market Value: $170

21
Curly™
Charlotte Sting
6/15/98 · LE-5,000
Market Value: $225

22
Curly™
Chicago Bears
12/20/98 · LE-10,000
Market Value: $120

23
Curly™
Cleveland Rockers
8/15/98 · LE-3,200
Market Value: $150

24
Curly™
New York Mets
8/22/98 · LE-30,000
Market Value: $95

25
Curly™
San Antonio Spurs
4/27/98 · LE-2,500
Market Value: $185

	Price Paid	Value of My Collection
14.		
15.		
16.		
17.		
18.		
19.		
20.		
21.		
22.		
23.		
24.		
25.		
26.		
27.		
28.		
29.		
30.		
31.		
32.		
33.		
34.		
35.		
36.		
37.		
38.		
39.		
40.		

26
Daisy™
Chicago Cubs
5/3/98 · LE-10,000
Market Value: $425

27
Derby™
Houston Astros
8/16/98 · LE-15,000
Market Value: $110

28
Derby™
Indianapolis Colts
10/4/98 · LE-10,000
Market Value: $120

29
Dotty™
Los Angeles Sparks
7/31/98 · LE-3,000
Market Value: $155

30
Ears™
Oakland A's
3/15/98 · LE-1,500
Market Value: $275

31
Glory™
All-Star Game
7/7/98 · LE-52,000 approx.
Market Value: $300

32
Gobbles™
Phoenix Coyotes
11/26/98 · LE-5,000
Market Value: N/E

33
Gobbles™
St. Louis Blues
11/24/98 · LE-7,500
Market Value: $90

34
Gracie™
Chicago Cubs
9/13/98 · LE-10,000
Market Value: $135

35
Hissy™
Arizona Diamondbacks
6/14/98 · LE-6,500
Market Value: $160

36
Lucky™
Minnesota Twins
7/31/98 · LE-10,000
Market Value: $120

37
Maple™
Canadian Special Olympics
8/97 & 12/97 · N/A
Market Value: $440

38
Mel™
Anaheim Angels
9/6/98 · LE-10,000
Market Value: $125

39
Mel™
Detroit Shock
7/25/98 · LE-5,000
Market Value: $140

40
Mystic™
Los Angeles Sparks
8/3/98 · LE-5,000
Market Value: $145

Value Totals _____

COLLECTOR'S
VALUE GUIDE™

VALUE GUIDE — SPORTS PROMOTION BEANIE BABIES®

41. Mystic™
Washington Mystics
7/11/98 · LE-5,000
Market Value: $165

42. Peanut™
Oakland A's
8/1/98 · LE-15,000
Market Value: $110

43. Peanut™
Oakland A's
9/6/98 · LE-15,000
Market Value: $110

44. Pinky™
San Antonio Spurs
4/29/98 · LE-2,500
Market Value: $215

45. Pinky™
Tampa Bay Devil Rays
8/23/98 · LE-10,000
Market Value: $95

46. Pugsly™
Atlanta Braves
9/2/98 · LE-12,000
Market Value: $90

47. Pugsly™
Texas Rangers
8/4/98 · LE-10,000
Market Value: $130

48. Roam™
Buffalo Sabres
2/19/99 · LE-5,000
Market Value: N/E

49. Roary™
Kansas City Royals
5/31/98 · LE-13,000
Market Value: $110

50. Rocket™
Toronto Blue Jays
9/6/98 · LE-12,000
Market Value: $150

51. Rover™
Cincinnati Reds
8/16/98 · LE-15,000
Market Value: $105

52. Scoop™
Houston Comets
8/6/98 · LE-5,000
Market Value: $185

53. Sly™
Arizona Diamondbacks
8/27/98 · LE-10,000
Market Value: $90

54. Smoochy™
St. Louis Cardinals
8/14/98 · LE-20,000
Market Value: $135

55. Spunky™
Buffalo Sabres
10/23/98 · LE-5,000
Market Value: $90

56. Stretch™
New York Yankees
8/9/98 · N/A
Market Value: $130

57. Stretch™
St. Louis Cardinals
5/22/98 · LE-20,000
Market Value: $135

58. Stripes™
Detroit Tigers
5/31/98 · LE-10,000
Market Value: $120

59. Stripes™
Detroit Tigers
8/8/98 · LE-10,000
Market Value: $110

60. Strut™
Indiana Pacers
4/2/98 · LE-5,000
Market Value: $130

61. Tuffy™
New Jersey Devils
10/24/98 · LE-5,000
Market Value: $90

62. Tuffy™
San Francisco Giants
8/30/98 · LE-10,000
Market Value: $105

63. Valentino™
Canadian Special Olympics
6/98, 9/98 & 10/98 · N/A
Market Value: $275

64. Valentino™
New York Yankees
5/17/98 · LE-10,000
Market Value: $280

65. Waddle™
Pittsburgh Penguins
10/24/98 · LE-7,000
Market Value: $85

66. Waddle™
Pittsburgh Penguins
11/21/98 · LE-7,000
Market Value: $85

67. Weenie™
Tampa Bay Devil Rays
7/26/98 · LE-15,000
Market Value: $115

SPORTS PROMOTION BEANIE BABIES®

	Price Paid	Value of My Collection
41.		
42.		
43.		
44.		
45.		
46.		
47.		
48.		
49.		
50.		
51.		
52.		
53.		
54.		
55.		
56.		
57.		
58.		
59.		
60.		
61.		
62.		
63.		
64.		
65.		
66.		
67.		

COLLECTOR'S VALUE GUIDE™

Value Totals _____

THE BEANIE BUDDIES® FAMILY GROWS AGAIN

A total of 14 new pieces joined their nine existing friends in the *Beanie Buddies* line on January 1, 1999. Four of the new releases have matching *Beanie Baby* counterparts that are currently available, while seven new *Beanie Buddies* are styled after *Beanie Babies* designs that have retired within the past year. In addition, two of the new pieces, "Chilly" the polar bear and "Peking" the panda, feature some of the most coveted retired *Beanie Babies* animals.

DEGREE OF DIFFICULTY RATINGS
Just Released
Easy To Find
Moderate To Find
Hard To Find
Very Hard To Find
Impossible To Find

1

Beak™

Kiwi · #9301
Issued: September 30, 1998
Current – Very Hard To Find

Market Value: $_____

Beanie Buddies® Fact
Beak the Beanie Baby
and Beak the Beanie Buddy
are the first to be released as a set!

Price Paid: $_____
Date Purchased: _____

Value
Totals _____

COLLECTOR'S
VALUE GUIDE™

2

NEW!

Bongo™

Monkey · #9312
Issued: January 1, 1999
Current – Just Released

Market Value: $_____

Beanie Buddies® Fact
Bongo the Beanie Baby
was first named Nana.
Ty Warner liked the name Bongo better
because he plays the Bongos!

F.Y.I.

Price Paid: $ 9.99
Date Purchased: may 24, 1999

3

NEW!

Bubbles™

Fish · #9323
Issued: January 1, 1999
Current – Just Released

Market Value: $_____

Beanie Buddies® Fact
Bubbles the Beanie Baby made
in the swimming position was
quite a challenge to manufacture.

F.Y.I.

Price Paid: $ 10.00
Date Purchased: april 24, 1999

4

NEW!

Chilly™

Polar Bear · #9317
Issued: January 1, 1999
Current – Just Released

Market Value: $_____

Price Paid: $ 9.99
Date Purchased: May 27, 1999

Beanie Buddies® Fact
Chilly the Beanie Baby
was introduced in June of 1994 and
retired in January of 1996 making
him one of the most sought after!

F.Y.I.

5

NEW!

Chip™

Cat · #9318
Issued: January 1, 1999
Current – Just Released

Market Value: $_____

Price Paid: $_____
Date Purchased: _____

Beanie Buddies® Fact
Chip the Beanie Baby
due to the variety of colors and pattern shapes,
is one of the most difficult to produce.
It takes over 20 pieces to make Chip!

F.Y.I.

Value
Totals _____

COLLECTOR'S
VALUE GUIDE™

6

NEW!

Erin™

Bear · #9309
Issued: January 1, 1999
Current – Just Released

Market Value: $_____

Beanie Buddies® Fact
Erin the Beanie Baby
is the first bear to represent a country
but not wear the country's flag!

F.Y.I.

Price Paid: $ 10.00
Date Purchased: June 18, 1999

7

NEW!

Hippity™

Bunny · #9324
Issued: January 1, 1999
Current – Just Released

Market Value: $_____

Beanie Buddies® Fact
Hippity the Beanie Baby
is a shade of green called Spring Mint.
Custom colors like Spring Mint are
difficult to maintain throughout production.

F.Y.I.

Price Paid: $ 10.00
Date Purchased: June 18, 1999

COLLECTOR'S
VALUE GUIDE™

Value
Totals _____

8

Humphrey™

Camel · #9307
Issued: September 30, 1998
Current – Impossible To Find

Market Value: $_____

Beanie Buddies® Fact
Humphrey the Beanie Baby
was one of the first to be retired.
Very few were produced,
making him highly collectable!

Price Paid: $ _10.00_
Date Purchased: _april 24, 1999_

9

Jake™

Mallard Duck · #9304
Issued: September 30, 1998
Current – Very Hard To Find

Market Value: $_____

Beanie Buddies® Fact
Jake the Beanie Baby
due to his numerous colors
was difficult to manufacture
making him one of the most sought after!

Price Paid: $ _9.99_
Date Purchased: _may 27, 1999_

Value
Totals _____

COLLECTOR'S
VALUE GUIDE™

10

NEW!

Patti™

Platypus · #9320
Issued: January 1, 1999
Current – Just Released

Market Value: $_____

Beanie Buddies® Fact
Patti the Beanie Baby
was one of the original nine.
Patti was available in both
maroon and magenta!

F.Y.I.

Price Paid: $ 9.99
Date Purchased: May 27, 1999

11

Peanut™

Elephant · #9300
Issued: September 30, 1998
Current – Impossible To Find

Market Value: $_____

Beanie Buddies® Fact
Peanut the Beanie Baby
made in this royal blue color
is extremely rare and very valuable!

F.Y.I.

Price Paid: $ 12.00
Date Purchased: June 11, 1999

12

NEW!

Peking™

Panda · #9310
Issued: January 1, 1999
Current - Just Released

Market Value: $_____

Beanie Buddies® Fact
Peking the Beanie Baby
was the first Panda made by Ty.
He was retired after only six months
making him highly collectible!

Price Paid: $ 9.99
Date Purchased: May 23, 1999

13

NEW!

Pinky™

Flamingo · #9316
Issued: January 1, 1999
Current - Just Released

Market Value: $_____

Beanie Buddies® Fact
Pinky the Beanie Baby
was a manufacturing challenge
because of her long neck!

Price Paid: $_____
Date Purchased: _____

Value
Totals _____

14

Quackers™

Duck · #9302
Issued: September 30, 1998
Current – Very Hard To Find

Market Value: $_____

Beanie Buddies® Fact
Quackers the Beanie Baby
retired in May 1998,
was once made without wings!

F.Y.I.

Price Paid: $ 9.99
Date Purchased: May 29, 1999

15

Rover™

Dog · #9305
Issued: September 30, 1998
Current – Very Hard To Find

Market Value: $_____

Beanie Buddies® Fact
Rover the Beanie Baby
was the first non-breed dog.
Introduced in the summer of 1996
this red color set him apart!

F.Y.I.

Price Paid: $ 10.00
Date Purchased: April 22, 1999

16

NEW!

Smoochy™

Frog • #9315
Issued: January 1, 1999
Current – Just Released

Market Value: $_____

Beanie Buddies® Fact
Smoochy the Beanie Baby
is the second Beanie Baby frog
made by Ty!

Price Paid: $ 9.99
Date Purchased: June 4, 1999

F.Y.I.

17

NEW!

Snort™

Bull • #9311
Issued: January 1, 1999
Current – Just Released

Market Value: $_____

Beanie Buddies® Fact
Snort the Beanie Baby
is the second bull made by Ty.
The first bull did not have hooves!

Price Paid: $ 11.00
Date Purchased: June 23, 1999

F.Y.I.

Value
Totals _____

COLLECTOR'S
VALUE GUIDE™

18

NEW!

Squealer™

Pig · #9313
Issued: January 1, 1999
Current – Just Released

Market Value: $_____

Beanie Buddies® Fact
Squealer the Beanie Baby
was one of the original nine.
Squealer was so popular that
he didn't retire for over four years!

Price Paid: $ _10.00_
Date Purchased: _June 11 1999_

F.Y.I.

19

Stretch™

Ostrich · #9303
Issued: September 30, 1998
Current – Very Hard To Find

Market Value: $_____

Beanie Buddies® Fact
Stretch the Beanie Baby
is one of the most difficult to produce
due to her long neck and numerous parts!

Price Paid: $_____
Date Purchased: _____

F.Y.I.

COLLECTOR'S
VALUE GUIDE™

Value
Totals _____

20

Teddy™

Bear · #9306
Issued: September 30, 1998
Current – Impossible To Find

Market Value: $_____

Beanie Buddies® Fact
Teddy the Beanie Baby
was made in six colors.
A very limited number were produced
in this special cranberry color!

Price Paid: $_____
Date Purchased: _____

F.Y.I.

21

NEW!

Tracker™

Basset Hound · #9319
Issued: January 1, 1999
Current – Just Released

Market Value: $_____

Beanie Buddies® Fact
Tracker the Beanie Baby
has the most expressive eyes.
Close attention to this detail
means limited production.

F.Y.I.

Price Paid: $ 9.99
Date Purchased: may 24 999

Value
Totals _____

COLLECTOR'S
VALUE GUIDE™

22

Twigs™

Giraffe · #9308
Issued: September 30, 1998
Retired: January 1, 1999

Market Value: $125

Beanie Buddies® Fact
Twigs the Beanie Baby
was manufactured in fabric
created exclusively for Ty
and was retired in May 1998!

Price Paid: $_____
Date Purchased: _____

23

NEW!

Waddle™

Penguin · #9314
Issued: January 1, 1999
Current – Just Released

Market Value: $_____

Beanie Buddies® Fact
Waddle the Beanie Baby
was the first of two penguins
to be made by Ty.
He was retired in April of 1998!

Price Paid: $ _9.99_
Date Purchased: _June 4, 1999_

7

Doby™
Doberman • 2nd Promotion, #1 of 12
Issued: May 22, 1998
Retired: June 12, 1998
Price Paid: $_____
Market Value: $15

8

Goldie™
Goldfish • 1st Promotion, #5 of 10
Issued: April 11, 1997
Retired: May 15, 1997
Price Paid: $_____
Market Value: $25

9

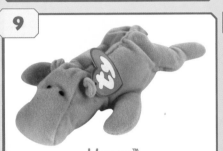

Happy™
Hippo • 2nd Promotion, #6 of 12
Issued: May 22, 1998
Retired: June 12, 1998
Price Paid: $_____
Market Value: $7

10

Inch™
Inchworm • 2nd Promotion, #4 of 12
Issued: May 22, 1998
Retired: June 12, 1998
Price Paid: $_____
Market Value: $7

11

Lizz™
Lizard • 1st Promotion, #10 of 10
Issued: April 11, 1997
Retired: May 15, 1997
Price Paid: $_____
Market Value: $20

12

Mel™
Koala • 2nd Promotion, #7 of 12
Issued: May 22, 1998
Retired: June 12, 1998
Price Paid: $_____
Market Value: $7

Value
Totals _____

COLLECTOR'S
VALUE GUIDE™

13

Patti™
Platypus · 1st Promotion, #1 of 10
Issued: April 11, 1997
Retired: May 15, 1997
Price Paid: $_____
Market Value: $38

14

Peanut™
Elephant · 2nd Promotion, #12 of 12
Issued: May 22, 1998
Retired: June 12, 1998
Price Paid: $_____
Market Value: $7

15

Pinchers™
Lobster · 2nd Promotion, #5 of 12
Issued: May 22, 1998
Retired: June 12, 1998
Price Paid: $_____
Market Value: $7

16

Pinky™
Flamingo · 1st Promotion, #2 of 10
Issued: April 11, 1997
Retired: May 15, 1997
Price Paid: $_____
Market Value: $50

17

Quacks™
Duck · 1st Promotion, #9 of 10
Issued: April 11, 1997
Retired: May 15, 1997
Price Paid: $_____
Market Value: $20

18

Scoop™
Pelican · 2nd Promotion, #8 of 12
Issued: May 22, 1998
Retired: June 12, 1998
Price Paid: $_____
Market Value: $7

COLLECTOR'S
VALUE GUIDE™

Value
Totals _____

19

Seamore™
Seal • 1st Promotion, #7 of 10
Issued: April 11, 1997
Retired: May 15, 1997
Price Paid: $_____
Market Value: $28

20

Snort™
Bull • 1st Promotion, #8 of 10
Issued: April 11, 1997
Retired: May 15, 1997
Price Paid: $_____
Market Value: $18

21

Speedy™
Turtle • 1st Promotion, #6 of 10
Issued: April 11, 1997
Retired: May 15, 1997
Price Paid: $_____
Market Value: $25

22

Twigs™
Giraffe • 2nd Promotion, #3 of 12
Issued: May 22, 1998
Retired: June 12, 1998
Price Paid: $_____
Market Value: $12

23

Waddle™
Penguin • 2nd Promotion, #11 of 12
Issued: May 22, 1998
Retired: June 12, 1998
Price Paid: $_____
Market Value: $8

24

Zip™
Cat • 2nd Promotion, #10 of 12
Issued: May 22, 1998
Retired: June 12, 1998
Price Paid: $_____
Market Value: $8

Value
Totals _____

COLLECTOR'S
VALUE GUIDE™

BEANIE BABIES® VALUE TOTALS

Page 27

Page 28

Page 29

Page 30

Page 31

Page 32

Page 33

Page 34

Page 35

Page 36

Page 37

Page 38

Page 39

Page 40

Page 41

Page 42

Page 43

Page 44

Page 45

Page 46

Page 47

BEANIE BABIES® VALUE TOTALS

Page 48

Page 49

Page 50

Page 51

Page 52

Page 53

Page 54

Page 55

Page 56

Page 57

Page 58

Page 59

Page 60

Page 61

Page 62

Page 63

Page 64

Page 65

Page 66

Page 67

BEANIE BABIES® VALUE TOTALS

Page 68

Page 69

Page 70

Page 71

Page 72

Page 73

Page 74

Page 75

Page 76

Page 77

Page 78

Page 79

Page 80

Page 81

Page 82

Page 83

Page 84

Page 85

Page 86

Page 87

Page 88

Page 89

TOTAL VALUE OF MY COLLECTION

BEANIE BABIES® *VALUE TOTALS*	BEANIE BABIES® *VALUE TOTALS*	BEANIE BUDDIES® *VALUE TOTALS*
Page 90	Page 111	Page 126
Page 91	Page 112	Page 127
Page 92	Page 113	Page 128
Page 93	Page 114	Page 129
Page 94	Page 115	Page 130
Page 95	Page 116	Page 131
Page 96	Page 117	Page 132
Page 97	Page 118	Page 133
Page 98	Page 119	Page 134
Page 99	Page 120	Page 135
Page 100	Page 121	Page 136
Page 101	Page 122	Page 137
Page 102	Subtotal	Page 138
Page 103		Subtotal
Page 104	SPORTS PROMOTION BEANIE BABIES® *VALUE TOTALS*	TEENIE BEANIE BABIES™ *VALUE TOTALS*
Page 105		Page 139
Page 106	Page 123	Page 140
Page 107	Page 124	Page 141
Page 108	Page 125	Page 142
Page 109	Subtotal	Subtotal
Page 110		

GRAND
TOTAL _____

COLLECTOR'S
VALUE GUIDE™

$\mathcal{I}$t's very unlikely that collectors knew what they had when they purchased the first *Beanie Babies*. For most, they were just cute toys for the kids. Before long, however, the noise of a distant storm could be heard coming through the collectibles landscape and soon a *Beanie Babies* frenzy was underway. Some of the early animals are now worth thousands of dollars; including "Chilly" the polar bear, "Humphrey" the camel and "Peking" the panda. That's hard to believe considering they sold in retail stores for less than $7. So what caused their values to soar? It's called the secondary market.

The secondary market is a system created when there's a continued demand for a product and not enough supply to meet that demand. Typically, collectibles on the secondary market are no longer available to collectors because they have been retired, are extremely hard to find in retail outlets or are no longer in production (as is the case with variations). In the case of the *Beanie Babies*, collectors are grabbing them up almost as soon as they hit store shelves, forcing some collectors to search elsewhere.

So where do you go to find the secondary market? There are all kinds of places you can find *Beanie Babies*. One of the most popular is the Internet. It's the newest and one of the most convenient ways to shop. You're just a click away from your favorite *Beanie Babies* without having to leave the comfort of your own home! On the Internet, you have access to *Beanie Babies* collectors from around the world and can contact both individuals and secondary market dealers (people who specialize in the buying, selling or trading of collectibles) to find all of the latest information.

The Internet is also home to numerous auction sites where you can read about, see pictures of, and bid on the *Beanie Babies* you want. However, if the Internet is the place you choose to buy your *Beanie Babies*, use caution – make sure the seller is reliable before sending him or her any money or disclosing your credit card information. (To learn more about *Beanie Babies* and the Internet, please turn to page 148.)

Other common places where *Beanie Babies* can be found include trade shows, classified ads, collector magazines and swap meets. Most retailers do not participate in the secondary market, but some may be able to act as a liaison between you and other collectors who share the same interests. Ask your favorite retailer if he or she has a list of other collectors looking to buy or sell certain pieces.

Now that you know where to find the secondary market, you may be wondering how it works. The importance of tag generations cannot be expressed enough when dealing with secondary market value. As a common rule, the earlier the swing tag is, the more valuable the piece becomes! Many collectors were unaware of *Beanie Babies* back in 1994 when the first introductions were released, making the earlier *Beanie Babies* more difficult to find today. The recently retired "Chocolate" the moose, one of the "Original Nine" with a fifth generation swing tag is currently valued at $13 in the Collector's Value Guide™. However, with his first generation swing tag, he's going for around $400.

Another reason some *Beanie Babies* are so high in value is because of design or color variations among the same style. For instance, "Peanut" was first issued in 1995 as a royal blue elephant. Just months later, his color was changed to light blue and the previous version was discontinued. Now, five years later, the royal blue "Peanut" is selling for about $5,000 on the secondary market because he is so rare.

If you are collecting with secondary market value in mind, remember that dirty *Beanie Babies* are often unwanted *Beanie Babies*. Keeping your *Beanie Babies* clean is a must if you are (or will be) in the market to sell. The most popular way of keeping your *Beanie Babies* free of dirt, dust, smoke or any kind of odor, is to store them in acrylic boxes. The boxes are clear and are made so that your special animal has all the room it needs to be comfortable. Avoid displaying them in direct sunlight, whether they are in a box or not. Many of them have bright, vibrant colors, and just like us, too much sun can have irreversible effects. If you do end up needing to wash a *Beanie Baby*, put it in a pillowcase for extra protection, and wash in mild detergent on the gentle cycle . . . and remember to remove the swing tag!

Whether buying or selling on the secondary market there are several things to consider in addition to the condition of the fabric, including the condition of the swing and tush tags. A swing tag in perfect condition with no creases or tears can add significantly to the value of the piece. On the other hand, the value of a *Beanie Baby* with a missing or damaged swing tag can drop dramatically from the price of one with a "mint" tag. If you are the seller, make sure you carefully note the condition of the tags or any other problems that you think the buyer may want to know.

The *Beanie Babies* craze is as strong as ever. Both children and adults are entranced by each and every one of them, making for the hottest secondary market in the world of collectibles. With this in mind, however, collect because you love to, not because you hope to make a profit. Remember that the *Beanie Babies* were created to bring joy and happiness to all their owners, no matter what the price!

The Internet

*F*or a line of stuffed animals to have their own web site is a treat. For *Beanie Babies*, it's a necessity. These understuffed beanbag animals have become the national craze of collectors since their introduction in 1994. But unlike most successful ventures that rise to the top with the help of advertising, *Beanie Babies* did it by word of mouth, and eventually, like almost everything else in the 1990s, the Internet.

Beanie Babies began appearing on the web during the summer of 1996. Ty Inc. created **www.ty.com** as an informational tool, offering up-to-date pictures of all the Ty lines. Adding to the site's allure is a diary that's written each month by the "Info Beanie." Sometimes the diary gives hints about upcoming *Beanie Baby* news but most often it is a fun glimpse of what life as a *Beanie Baby* is like. A "members only" area called "The Beanie Connection" lets you know fun facts like when your favorite *Beanie Babies*' birthdays are approaching. From here, you can also get connected with other collectors, or maybe find an Internet pen pal. For members of Ty's Beanie Babies® Official Club™, there's another site just for you! The fun part about this area is that members get privileged information before it's available to the public. There are also pictures to color, games to play and general information about the club itself.

The Ty Inc. web site is certainly not the only place collectors can learn about the pocket-sized wonders. If you type *"Beanie Babies"* in the various search engines available, you'll have a hard time actually choosing which web site to visit first. There are virtually hundreds of sites, many of which are dedicated to *Beanie Babies* alone. Some are a collector's page of pictures, while others are extremely detailed sites with pictures, descriptions, news, and even *Beanie Babies* gossip. Web-goers beware, however, as you can't always believe everything you see on the Internet.

The Internet has also become a spot where many collectors buy *Beanie Babies*. Some retailers and secondary market dealers have web pages where you can browse. You can usually order the *Beanie Babies* right from your computer – it's shopping made easy! If this is your way of buying your *Beanie Babies* remember to use caution. Make sure the retailer or individual is legitimate before sending them any personal information or money.

Another Internet option that has gained popularity are auction sites. It's here that you can bid on probably every *Beanie Baby* made. Individuals put their *Beanie Babies* up for sale; including descriptions and, sometimes, a picture of the animal you'll be receiving if you are the highest bidder. Auction sites can be a good place to find *Beanie Babies* because they generally sell for less than if you were to buy them from a collector "in person."

Since their inception, *Beanie Babies* have come from being a toy not available in toy stores to being, perhaps, the top selling collectible ever. Now, thanks to computers, the *Beanie Baby* frenzy has grown and the Internet has become one of the most traveled routes for collectors of all ages.

THE HOTTEST SITE AROUND!

www.collectorbee.com

Be sure to check out all of the latest news about Ty's *Beanie Babies* on our new web site, www.collectorbee.com.

You'll find the most updated information about new releases, retirements and the latest scoop on not just all your favorite Ty lines, but the rest of the collectibles industry as well.

Variations

*B*eanie Babies have taken the collecting world by storm. Since being introduced in 1994, these pint-sized beanbag animals have taken over the collectibles market, causing a craze like no other.

Once a collection like *Beanie Babies* becomes so large and so popular, it's only a matter of time before collectors begin noticing "variations" to pieces they have. The word "variation" is quite broad. It can mean anything from an intentional change like a piece's name or a new design; to a mistake or error during production, such as a misspelled word or an ear that's sewn on backwards. Although most slight variations don't affect the secondary market value of a piece, several well-known (but hard to find) variations are among the most valuable pieces in the collection.

NAME CHANGES

Brownie™/Cubbie™

It's the same bear, just different names. The bear's first name, "Brownie," went into permanent hibernation soon after he was released in 1994. He was re-named "Cubbie" and kept that name until he retired in 1997.

Creepy™/Spinner™

At first glance, "Creepy" seems like the perfect name for this *Beanie Baby* spider. But even so, when the "Creepy" name appeared on his tush tag, it was actually a mistake . . . this creature's real name has always been "Spinner."

Doodle™/Strut™

This proud Beanie liked to "Strut" around so much, Ty changed his name to just that in 1997, making the "Doodle" version available for only a few short months.

Doodle™ style 4171
DATE OF BIRTH : 3 - 8 - 96
Listen closely to "cock-a-doodle-doo"
What's the rooster saying to you?
Hurry, wake up sleepy head
We have lots to do, get out of bed!

Visit our web page!!!
http://www.ty.com

Strut™ style 4171
DATE OF BIRTH : 3 - 8 - 96
Listen closely to "cock-a-doodle-doo"
What's the rooster saying to you?
Hurry, wake up sleepy head
We have lots to do, get out of bed!

Visit our web page!!!
http://www.ty.com

Nana™/Bongo™

"Monkey see, monkey do." When "Nana" noticed fellow Beanie Babies changing their names, he wanted to, as well! So, in 1995, he took on the new name of "Bongo."

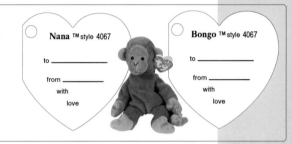

Nana™ style 4067
to _____
from _____
with
love

Bongo™ style 4067
to _____
from _____
with
love

Pride™/Maple™

"Pride" didn't stop this adorable Canadian bear from joining in and changing his name. But it will take a very lucky collector to find him with "Pride" on his tush tag. His name was changed to "Maple" just prior to his release in 1997.

The Beanie Babies Collection™
ty
Pride
HAND MADE IN CHINA
© 1996 TY INC.
OAKBROOK IL, U.S.A.
SURFACE WASHABLE
ALL NEW MATERIAL
POLYESTER FIBER
& P.V.C. PELLETS CE
REG. NO PA. 1965(KR)

The Beanie Babies Collection™
★ **ty**
Maple
HAND MADE IN CHINA
© 1996 TY INC.
OAKBROOK IL, U.S.A.
SURFACE WASHABLE
ALL NEW MATERIAL
POLYESTER FIBER
& P.V.C. PELLETS CE
REG. NO PA. 1965(KR)

Punchers™/Pinchers™

Is it a name change or a whole different lobster? "Punchers" appeared on the first generation of "Pinchers" tags and although some say that "Punchers" has bigger claws than his look-alike, most believe the different name is just an error.

The Beanie Babies Collection
Punchers™ style 4026
© 1993 Ty Inc. Oakbrook, IL. USA
All Rights Reserved. Caution:
Remove this tag before giving
toy to a child. For ages 5 and up.
Handmade in Korea.
Surface
Wash.

The Beanie Babies Collection
Pinchers™ style 4026
© 1993 Ty Inc. Oakbrook, IL. USA
All Rights Reserved. Caution:
Remove this tag before giving
toy to a child. For ages 5 and up.
Handmade in Korea.
Surface
Wash.

VARIATIONS

Spook™/Spooky™

Collectors didn't find this change scary at all. Early on, this friendly ghost's tag was spotted reading "Spook," but before collectors could say "Boo!" all of the ghosts with incorrect tags had been snatched up leaving only the corrected "Spooky" in stores.

Tuck™/Tusk™

A spelling error on this little guy caused some confusion during 1996. "Tusk" was halfway through his life when some of his fourth generation tags began saying "Tuck."

COLOR CHANGES

Batty™ – This bat was tired of no one noticing him in the dark, so he decided to brighten things up. "Batty" changed his fabric from his original brownish color to a more standout tie-dye in late 1998. As of early 1999, the tie-dye version was still hard to find!

Digger™:

Perhaps this little crab spent too much time digging in the sand during the sunny days of the summer of 1995. That's when her shell's original orange color turned bright red.

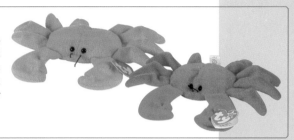

Happy™:

It's hard to be happy when you're so gray and "Happy" the hippo realized this shortly after joining his *Beanie Baby* friends. So, in mid-1995, he did something about it and spent the next three years decked out in cheerful lavender.

Inky™:

Friends in the deep blue sea thought this octopus' tan color was too drab for life under water so they ordered a color change. Now, everyone can spot "Inky" when he swims by in his new shade of pink! The tan version of "Inky" can also be found without a mouth.

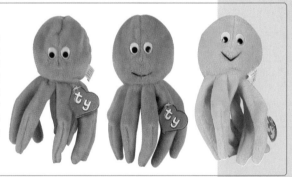

Lizzy™:

This lizard completely changed her look in 1996. After spending several months dressed in a tie-dyed outfit, she decided to change to black spots with a blue background, in addition to an orange and yellow belly.

VARIATIONS

Patti™: "Patti" loves change, but doesn't like to stray too far from what's familiar. A little over a year after she was released with a maroon color she began showing up a little brighter in a shade of magenta. Perhaps it was time to take the attention away from her beak!

Peanut™: Working for peanuts takes on a whole new meaning when you're talking about the royal blue "Peanut." Collectors will do just about anything to get their hands on this highly sought after elephant as only a handful were released before her color was changed to the intended light blue.

DESIGN CHANGES

Bongo™:
Monkeys are known to do whatever it takes to get attention and "Bongo" is no exception. As if his name change from "Nana" was not enough, he also changed the color of his tail from brown to tan.

Derby™:   The *Beanie Baby* stable is getting quite full from all of the different versions of "Derby" the horse.   The galloping herd of variations for this *Beanie Baby* goes from a fine mane, to a coarse mane, to a star on his forehead, to his new "fluffy" mane.

Iggy™:   When "Iggy" was first introduced, he was rainbow-colored.   The fact that there was another "lizard-type" *Beanie Baby* named "Rainbow" led collectors to believe "Iggy" had the wrong tags.   Later, "Iggy" began sticking his tongue out and then finally changed colors to the dark blue and green color that "Rainbow" had when he was first introduced.   Apparently it was just a case of switched fabric all along.

Inch™:

This little worm inched his way into the *Beanie Babies* variations when he turned up with new antennas.   In the middle of 1996, they were changed from felt to yarn, and remained so until he retired two years later.

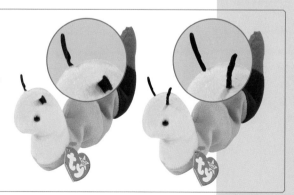

VARIATIONS

Lucky™: Seeing lots of spots is not unusual for this little lady. As a matter of fact, she considers herself "Lucky" for all the attention they have brought. She started out with just seven, then 21 and, finally, for the next year and a half she had 11!

Magic™:
Breathing fire all the time had turned the threads in this dragon's wings hot pink. The change didn't last long . . . after several months, the stitching on "Magic" returned to the light pink threads she'd had since birth!

Mystic™: Once upon a time there was only one version of this unicorn. "Mystic" first appeared with a fine mane and a tan horn in 1994, but then she changed her mane to coarse, and later her horn became iridescent. Now, "Mystic" is appearing with another fine, "fluffy" mane that's rainbow-colored. After all, anything's possible in the land of magic.

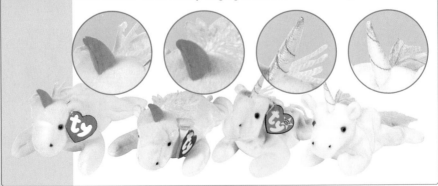

Nip™ and Zip™:

These two frisky felines came together to keep collectors guessing. Although they're two different colors, they both went through the same changes of a white face and tummy, to a solid-colored body, to having white boots on their paws.

Quackers™:

Believe it or not, this yellow fellow got around the first few months of his life without wings! Although he finally received his wings in 1995, the wingless version of "Quackers" is very popular . . . one would even say he's a lucky duck!

Rainbow™:

At the end of every "Rainbow" is a pot of gold. This "Rainbow," however, has given collectors much confusion about his identity. In fact, when he was first introduced he wasn't rainbow-colored at all, but a dark blue-green. Now, however, he has a more fitting rainbow-colored tie-dye coat, plus a new tongue.

Variations

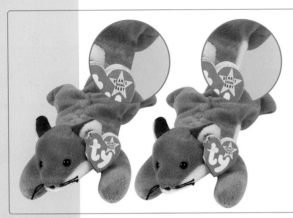

Sly™:

The chase was back on for this fox just months after his release. The change from a solid-colored belly to his new white belly was an easy one to spot and sent collectors embarking on a new fox hunt.

Spot™:

See "Spot" run . . . to actually get a spot! That's right – when this pup was first released, he just wasn't true to his name. So, after just three months of being "spotless," Ty added a black spot to his back, and kept the dog quite happy for the next three years.

Stripes™: Unlike most tigers, this little guy was tired of not being noticed! So, to attract more attention, he changed his dark color and thick stripes to a bright orange, with thinner black markings. Also, included in his metamorphosis was a fabric change that added a "fuzzy belly" to some of the early, darker versions.

Tank™:

"Tank" is a very determined armadillo. He was first released in 1996 without a shell and only seven "plates" to protect him. Soon, he decided that wasn't enough and he added two more plates. Then, almost a year before he retired, he fine-tuned his look to add horizontal stitches that completed his top-quality shell!

Teddy™:

The love for these adorable bears in six different colors doubled when each one changed its look. Released in the summer of 1995, the bears had eyes that were set far apart and noses set high on their faces. Then, after the new year, they emerged with face lifts that brought their nose farther down and eyes closer together.

INTERNAL CHANGES

Princess™:

They say that it's what's inside that counts, and that seems to hold true for "Princess." As the tush tags point out, some of these pieces are stuffed with "P.V.C." pellets and others with "P.E." pellets (which is also common with other *Beanie Babies*). Collectors seem to favor the earlier "P.V.C." version of this royal bear.

The Beanie Babies Collection®	The Beanie Babies Collection®
★ ty®	★ ty®
Princess™	Princess™
HANDMADE IN CHINA	HANDMADE IN CHINA
© 1997 TY INC.,	© 1997 TY INC.,
OAKBROOK, IL. U.S.A.	OAKBROOK, IL. U.S.A.
SURFACE WASHABLE	SURFACE WASHABLE
ALL NEW MATERIAL	ALL NEW MATERIAL
POLYESTER FIBER & P.V.C. PELLETS CE	POLYESTER FIBER & P.E. PELLETS CE
REG. NO PA. 1965(KR)	REG. NO PA. 1965(KR)

C ounterfeit beanbag toys began invading the *Beanie Babies* scene in 1996 and today pose a serious – and potentially expensive – problem for uninformed collectors. These forgeries are frequently sold on the Internet and include some valuable retirees.

Unfortunately, many people don't know they've bought – and are now selling – fakes. If you're buying *Beanie Babies* on the secondary market, try to become as educated as possible and know exactly what genuine *Beanie Babies* look and feel like.

Beanie Babies are currently made in more than 100 factories in the Far East; however, a few pieces reportedly are stolen from every shipment that leaves the factories en route to America. Even so, only about 20 percent of the *Beanie Babies* sold on the "Black Market," (which is particularly strong in Beijing, the capitol of China) are real – albeit stolen – since *Beanie Babies* cannot be legally sold in China. While some *Beanie Babies* sold in China may be factory rejects that did not meet Ty's strict quality control standards, the majority are turning out to be fakes.

The earliest knock-offs were often poor imitations. Then, as collectors became more knowledgeable about the details of both the toys and their tags, counterfeiters began producing more sophisticated clones. Today, collectors can find some remarkably accurate fake *Beanie Babies* on the secondary market, but closer inspection reveals that they aren't the "real McCoy."

Typically, counterfeit *Beanie Babies* have more than one noticeable problem (which should not be confused with variations of authentic Ty *Beanie Babies*), including any of the following:

Tag errors — Fake swing tags may be smaller or have uneven gold rims. Some are printed on laminated paper and the red and gold inks may bleed, fade or flake off. Sometimes the writing is too dark, washed out, smudged or contains spelling errors. Also, the spacing between words and lines may not match authentic tags and the plastic attachments

COUNTERFEIT

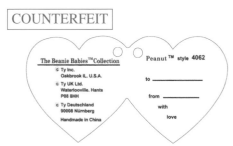

The Beanie Babies™Collection

Peanut ™ style 4062

ⓒ Ty Inc.
Oakbrook IL. U.S.A.

ⓒ Ty UK Ltd.
Waterlooville. Hants
P08 8HH

ⓒ Ty Deutschland
90008 Nürnberg

Handmade in China

to _____

from _____

with

love

are much longer. One dark blue "Peanut" imitation has a swing tag with letters spaced too far apart, and the "c" in the copyright symbol (ⓒ) is in bold type while the circle around it is not. Also, fake tush tags may be wider than the real ones.

Poor quality — The fabrics used on counterfeits may be shinier or have a rough grain that appears "nubby," especially if rubbed in the wrong direction. The stitching may be sloppy and inconsistent in size or spacing. The fabric on a fake "Brownie," for example, is often too rough, has a coarse nap and is darker than the original.

Wrong colors — Closely compare colors with genuine *Beanie Babies*; if a piece looks too light, too dark or just plain strange (such as a mint-green "Quackers" or a red "Pinky"), it may be wise to treat it as a counterfeit.

Four Tips For Buying On The Secondary Market

1. Know who you are buying from and always use extreme caution. Always purchase from an authorized Ty dealer or a collector with a reliable record.

2. Compare what you plan to purchase with an authentic version that was purchased from an authorized Ty dealer, not from the secondary market.

3. Tell the seller you wish to have the piece appraised and that if it is not genuine, you expect a full refund. Put this agreement in writing.

4. Get a written receipt for each purchase.

COUNTERFEIT ALERT!

Incorrect size, weight & shape — Fake *Beanie Babies* may be larger or smaller in size (and heavier or lighter in weight) than their real counterparts, or they may have too many or too few pellets. P.V.C. and P.E. pellets should be small and round, not large and cylindrically-shaped. Legs may appear too long or too short and the *Beanie Baby* may be misshapen. For example, one counterfeit "Peking" has ears that are more square, a nose that is wider and elongated and pellets that are much bigger than the real *Beanie Baby*.

Inaccurate details — The *Beanie Babies'* noses vary in size and color, so check with a reliable source before buying. Also, real *Beanie Babies* typically have small, shiny plastic eyes, while fake ones may have eyes that are the wrong size and appear dull. So again, it pays to know what the real *Beanie Babies* look like. Always check the size, color and quality of embroidery and sewn-on details. For example, one fake "Slither" has a tongue that is not only shorter than the authentic *Beanie Baby*, but inaccurately forked into a "V" shape. Also, neck ribbons should not be sewn on and should be a shiny satin on both sides. One imitation "Princess" comes with a ribbon of poor quality material that is only shiny on one side.

AUTHENTIC

COUNTERFEIT

Protecting yourself involves a little homework, but no one wants to pay top-dollar prices for worthless fakes. Becoming an educated consumer and taking the time to check out what you're really buying can save you a lot of money and heartache, and, in the end, will definitely pay off.

JANUARY Birthdays

Jan. 1, 1999 . . . Millenium™
Jan. 2, 1998 . . . . . . Zero™
Jan. 3, 1993 . . . . . . Spot™
Jan. 5, 1997 . . . . . . Kuku™
Jan. 6, 1993 . . . . . Patti™
Jan. 13, 1996 . . . . Crunch™
Jan. 14, 1997 . . . . Spunky™
Jan. 15, 1996 . . . . . . Mel™
Jan. 17, 1998 . . . Slippery™
Jan. 18, 1994 . . . . Bones™
Jan. 21, 1996 . . . . . Nuts™
Jan. 25, 1995 . . . . Peanut™
Jan. 26, 1996 . . . . . Chip™

FEBRUARY Birthdays

Feb. 1, 1996 . . . . . Peace™
Feb. 3, 1998 . . . . . . Beak™
Feb. 4, 1997 . . . . . Fetch™
Feb. 13, 1995 . . . . . Pinky™
Feb. 13, 1995 . . . . Stinky™
Feb. 14, 1994 . . . Valentino™
Feb. 14, 1998 . . . Valentina™
Feb. 17, 1996 . . . . . Baldy™
Feb. 19, 1998 . . . Prickles™
Feb. 20, 1996 . . . . Roary™
Feb. 20, 1997 . . . . . Early™
Feb. 22, 1995 . . . . . Tank™
Feb. 25, 1994 . . . Happy™
Feb. 27, 1996 . . . . Sparky™
Feb. 28, 1995 . . . . . . Flip™

MARCH Birthdays

March 1, 1998	Ewey™
March 2, 1995	Coral™
March 6, 1994	Nip™
March 8, 1996	Doodle™
March 8, 1996	Strut™
March 12, 1997	Rocket™
March 14, 1994	Ally™
March 17, 1997	Erin™
March 19, 1996	Seaweed™
March 20, 1997	Early™
March 21, 1996	Fleece™
March 23, 1998	Hope™
March 28, 1994	Zip™
March 29, 1998	Loosy™

APRIL Birthdays

April 3, 1996	Hoppity™
April 4, 1997	Hissy™
April 5, 1997	Whisper™
April 6, 1998	Nibbler™
April 7, 1997	Gigi™
April 10, 1998	Eggbert™
April 12, 1996	Curly™
April 16, 1997	Jake™
April 18, 1995	Ears™
April 19, 1994	Quackers™
April 23, 1993	Squealer™
April 25, 1993	Legs™
April 27, 1993	Chocolate™

MAY Birthdays

May 1, 1995 . . . . . Lucky™
May 1, 1996 . . . . Wrinkles™
May 2, 1996 . . . . . Pugsly™
May 3, 1996 . . . . . Chops™
May 4, 1998 . . . . . Hippie™
May 7, 1998 . . . . . Nibbly™
May 10, 1994 . . . . . Daisy™
May 11, 1995 . . . . . Lizzy™
May 13, 1993 . . . . . Flash™
May 15, 1995 . . . . Snort™
May 15, 1995 . . . Tabasco™
May 19, 1995 . . . . Twigs™
May 21, 1994 . . . . Mystic™
May 27, 1998 . . . . . Scat™
May 28, 1996 . . . . Floppity™
May 29, 1998 . . . . Canyon™
May 30, 1996 . . . . . Rover™
May 31, 1997 . . . . . Wise™

JUNE Birthdays

June 1, 1996 . . . . Hippity™
June 3, 1996 . . . . Freckles™
June 3, 1996 . . . . Scottie™
June 5, 1997 . . . . Tracker™
June 8, 1995 . . . . . Bucky™
June 8, 1995 . . . . . Manny™
June 10, 1998 . . . . . Mac™
June 11, 1995 . . . Stripes™
June 15, 1996 . . . . Scottie™
June 15, 1998 . . . . . Luke™
June 16, 1998 . . . . Stilts™
June 17, 1996 . . . . Gracie™
June 19, 1993 . . . Pinchers™
June 23, 1998 . . . . Sammy™
June 27, 1995 . . . . Bessie™

JULY Birthdays

July 1, 1996 . . . . . Maple™
July 1, 1996 . . . . . Scoop™
July 2, 1995 . . . . Bubbles™
July 4, 1996 . . . . . . Lefty™
July 4, 1996 . . . . . Righty™
July 4, 1997 . . . . . . Glory™
July 7, 1998 . . . . . Clubby™
July 8, 1993 . . . . . Splash™
July 14, 1995 . . . . . Ringo™
July 15, 1994 . . . . Blackie™
July 19, 1995 . . . . . Grunt™
July 20, 1995 . . . . Weenie™
July 23, 1998 . . . . . Fuzz™
July 28, 1996 . . . Freckles™
July 31, 1998 . . . . Scorch™

AUGUST Birthdays

Aug. 1, 1995 . . . . . Garcia™
Aug. 1, 1998 . . . . . Mooch™
Aug. 9, 1995 . . . . . . Hoot™
Aug. 12, 1997 . . . . . Iggy™
Aug. 13, 1996 . . . . . Spike™
Aug. 14, 1994 . . . . Speedy™
Aug. 16, 1998 . . . . . Kicks™
Aug. 17, 1995 . . . . Bongo™
Aug. 23, 1995 . . . . Digger™
Aug. 27, 1995 . . . . . Sting™
Aug. 28, 1997 . . . . Pounce™
Aug. 31, 1998 . . . . . Halo™

SEPTEMBER Birthdays

Sept. 3, 1995	Inch™
Sept. 3, 1996	Claude™
Sept. 5, 1995	Magic™
Sept. 8, 1998	Tiny™
Sept. 9, 1997	Bruno™
Sept. 12, 1996	Sly™
Sept. 16, 1995	Derby™
Sept. 16, 1995	Kiwi™
Sept. 18, 1995	Tusk™
Sept. 21, 1997	Stretch™
Sept. 27, 1998	Roam™
Sept. 29, 1997	Stinger™

OCTOBER Birthdays

Oct. 1, 1997	Smoochy™
Oct. 2, 1998	Butch™
Oct. 3, 1996	Bernie™
Oct. 3, 1998	Germania™
Oct. 9, 1996	Doby™
Oct. 10, 1997	Jabber™
Oct. 12, 1996	Tuffy™
Oct. 14, 1997	Rainbow™
Oct. 16, 1995	Bumble™
Oct. 17, 1996	Dotty™
Oct. 22, 1996	Snip™
Oct. 28, 1996	Spinner™
Oct. 29, 1996	Batty™
Oct. 30, 1995	Radar™
Oct. 31, 1995	Spooky™
Oct. 31, 1998	Pumkin'™

BEANIE BABIES® BIRTHDAYS

NOVEMBER

Nov. 3, 1997	Puffer™
Nov. 4, 1998	Goatee™
Nov. 6, 1996	Pouch™
Nov. 7, 1997	Ants™
Nov. 9, 1996	Congo™
Nov. 14, 1993	Cubbie™
Nov. 14, 1994	Goldie™
Nov. 18, 1998	Goochy™
Nov. 20, 1997	Prance™
Nov. 21, 1996	Nanook™
Nov. 27, 1996	Gobbles™
Nov. 28, 1995	Teddy™ (brown)
Nov. 29, 1994	Inky™

DECEMBER

Dec. 2, 1996	Jolly™
Dec. 6, 1997	Fortune™
Dec. 6, 1998	Santa™
Dec. 8, 1996	Waves™
Dec. 12, 1996	Blizzard™
Dec. 14, 1996	Seamore™
Dec. 15, 1997	Britannia™
Dec. 16, 1995	Velvet™
Dec. 19, 1995	Waddle™
Dec. 21, 1996	Echo™
Dec. 22, 1996	Snowball™
Dec. 24, 1995	Ziggy™
Dec. 25, 1996	1997 Teddy™
Dec. 25, 1998	1998 Teddy™

On this handy list, you can check off which Beanie Babies are in your collection. You can also circle the numbered heart that corresponds with the tag that your Beanie Baby is wearing. Current pieces are listed first, followed by retired pieces, and each variation is listed seperately.

Current Beanie Babies®

- ❑ 1999 Signature Bear™. ❺
- ❑ Batty™ (tie-dye) ...... ❺
- ❑ Beak™ .... ❺
- ❑ Britannia™ .... ❺
- ❑ Butch™ .... ❺
- ❑ Canyon™ .... ❺
- ❑ Chip™ .... ❹ ❺
- ❑ Clubby™ .... ❺
- ❑ Derby™ (star/fluffy mane) ... ❺
- ❑ Early™ .... ❺
- ❑ Eggbert™ .... ❺
- ❑ Erin™ .... ❺
- ❑ Ewey™ .... ❺
- ❑ Fortune™ .... ❺
- ❑ Fuzz™ .... ❺
- ❑ Germania™ .... ❺
- ❑ Gigi™ .... ❺
- ❑ Goatee™ .... ❺
- ❑ Gobbles™ .... ❹ ❺
- ❑ Goochy™ .... ❺
- ❑ Halo™ .... ❺
- ❑ Hippy™ .... ❺
- ❑ Hissy™ .... ❺

- ❑ Hope™ .... ❺
- ❑ Iggy™ (blue/no tongue) ❺
- ❑ Jabber™ .... ❺
- ❑ Jake™ .... ❺
- ❑ Kicks™ .... ❺
- ❑ Kuku™ .... ❺
- ❑ Loosy™ .... ❺
- ❑ Luke™ .... ❺
- ❑ Mac™ .... ❺
- ❑ Maple™ ("Maple™" tush tag) ❹ ❺
- ❑ Mel™ .... ❹ ❺
- ❑ Millenium™ .... ❺
- ❑ Mooch™ .... ❺
- ❑ Mystic™ (iridescent horn/fluffy mane).... ❺
- ❑ Nanook™ .... ❹ ❺
- ❑ Nibbler™ .... ❺
- ❑ Nibbly™ .... ❺
- ❑ Peace™ .... ❹ ❺
- ❑ Pouch™ .... ❹ ❺
- ❑ Pounce™ .... ❺
- ❑ Prance™ .... ❺
- ❑ Prickles™ .... ❺
- ❑ Princess™ (P.E. pellets). ❹
- ❑ Pugsly™ .... ❹ ❺
- ❑ Rainbow™ (tie-dye/tongue) ..... ❺
- ❑ Roam™ .... ❺
- ❑ Rocket™ .... ❺
- ❑ Sammy™ .... ❺
- ❑ Scat™ .... ❺
- ❑ Scorch™ .... ❺
- ❑ Slippery™ .... ❺
- ❑ Smoochy™ .... ❺
- ❑ Spunky™ .... ❺
- ❑ Stilts™ .... ❺
- ❑ Stretch™ .... ❺
- ❑ Strut™ .... ❹ ❺
- ❑ Tiny™ .... ❺
- ❑ Tracker™ .... ❺

- ❑ Valentina™ .... ❺
- ❑ Whisper™ .... ❺

Retired Beanie Babies®

- ❑ #1 Bear™ ..... Special Tag
- ❑ 1997 Teddy™ .... ❹
- ❑ 1998 Holiday Teddy™ . ❺
- ❑ Ally™ .... ❶ ❷ ❸ ❹
- ❑ Ants™ .... ❺
- ❑ Baldy™ .... ❹ ❺
- ❑ Batty™ (brown) .... ❹ ❺
- ❑ Bernie™ .... ❹ ❺
- ❑ Bessie™ .... ❸ ❹
- ❑ Billionaire Bear™ .... Special Tag
- ❑ Blackie™ .. ❶ ❷ ❸ ❹ ❺
- ❑ Blizzard™ .... ❹ ❺
- ❑ Bones™ ... ❶ ❷ ❸ ❹ ❺
- ❑ Bongo™ (tan tail) ❸ ❹ ❺
- ❑ Bongo™ (brown tail) ❸ ❹
- ❑ Bronty™ .... ❸
- ❑ Brownie™ .... ❶
- ❑ Bruno™ .... ❺
- ❑ Bubbles™ .... ❸ ❹
- ❑ Bucky™ .... ❸ ❹
- ❑ Bumble™ .... ❸ ❹
- ❑ Caw™ .... ❸
- ❑ Chilly™ .... ❶ ❷ ❸
- ❑ Chocolate™ ❶ ❷ ❸ ❹ ❺
- ❑ Chops™ .... ❸ ❹
- ❑ Claude™ .... ❹ ❺
- ❑ Congo™ .... ❹ ❺
- ❑ Coral™ .... ❸ ❹
- ❑ Crunch™ .... ❹ ❺
- ❑ Cubbie™ .. ❶ ❷ ❸ ❹ ❺
- ❑ Curly™ .... ❹ ❺
- ❑ Daisy™ ... ❶ ❷ ❸ ❹ ❺
- ❑ Derby™ (star/coarse mane) ... ❺
- ❑ Derby™ (no star/coarse mane) ...... ❸ ❹

- ☐ Derby™
  (no star/fine mane)... ❸
- ☐ Digger™ (red)...... ❸ ❹
- ☐ Digger™ (orange)❶ ❷ ❸
- ☐ Doby™ .... ❹ ❺
- ☐ Doodle™............ ❹
- ☐ Dotty™.......... ❹ ❺
- ☐ Ears™......... ❸ ❹ ❺
- ☐ Echo™............ ❹ ❺
- ☐ Fetch™............. ❺
- ☐ Flash™...... ❶ ❷ ❸ ❹
- ☐ Fleece™.......... ❹ ❺
- ☐ Flip™............. ❸ ❹
- ☐ Floppity™........ ❹ ❺
- ☐ Flutter™........... ❸
- ☐ Freckles™......... ❹ ❺
- ☐ Garcia™.......... ❸ ❹
- ☐ Glory™............ ❺
- ☐ Goldie™... ❶ ❷ ❸ ❹ ❺
- ☐ Gracie™.......... ❹ ❺
- ☐ Grunt™.......... ❸ ❹
- ☐ Happy™ (lavender)❸ ❹ ❺
- ☐ Happy™ (gray)... ❶ ❷ ❸
- ☐ Hippity™......... ❹ ❺
- ☐ Hoot™........... ❸ ❹
- ☐ Hoppity™........ ❹ ❺
- ☐ Humphrey™.... ❶ ❷ ❸
- ☐ Iggy™
  (tie-dye/tongue)..... ❺
- ☐ Iggy™
  (tie-dye/no tongue)... ❺
- ☐ Inch™
  (yarn antennas).... ❹ ❺
- ☐ Inch™
  (felt antennas).... ❸ ❹
- ☐ Inky™ (pink).... ❸ ❹ ❺
- ☐ Inky™ (tan/mouth). ❷ ❸
- ☐ Inky™
  (tan/no mouth).... ❶ ❷
- ☐ Jolly™............ ❹ ❺
- ☐ Kiwi™ .... ❸ ❹
- ☐ Lefty™............ ❹
- ☐ Legs™...... ❶ ❷ ❸ ❹
- ☐ Libearty™.......... ❹

- ☐ Lizzy™ (blue)... ❸ ❹ ❺
- ☐ Lizzy™ (tie-dye)...... ❸
- ☐ Lucky™ (11 spots)... ❹ ❺
- ☐ Lucky™ (21 spots)..... ❹
- ☐ Lucky™ (7 spots)❶ ❷ ❸
- ☐ Magic™
  (pale pink thread). ❸ ❹
- ☐ Magic™
  (hot pink thread)..... ❹
- ☐ Manny™.......... ❸ ❹
- ☐ Maple™
  ("Pride™" tush tag).... ❹
- ☐ Mystic™ (iridescent .....
  horn/coarse mane). ❹ ❺
- ☐ Mystic™ (brown
  horn/coarse mane). ❸ ❹
- ☐ Mystic™ (brown
  horn/fine mane) ❶ ❷ ❸
- ☐ Nana™ .... ❸
- ☐ Nip™ (white paws)❸ ❹ ❺
- ☐ Nip™ (all gold) .... ❸
- ☐ Nip™ (white face).. ❷ ❸
- ☐ Nuts™............ ❹ ❺
- ☐ Patti™ (magenta) ❸ ❹ ❺
- ☐ Patti™ (maroon). ❶ ❷ ❸
- ☐ Peanut™ (light blue)❸ ❹ ❺
- ☐ Peanut™ (dark blue)... ❸
- ☐ Peking™ .... ❶ ❷ ❸
- ☐ Pinchers™ ("Pinchers™"
  swing tag)❶ ❷ ❸ ❹ ❺
- ☐ Pinchers™ ("Punchers™"
  swing tag) .... ❶
- ☐ Pinky™ .... ❸ ❹ ❺
- ☐ Princess™
  (P.V.C. pellets) .... ❹
- ☐ Puffer™ .... ❺
- ☐ Pumkin'™ .... ❺
- ☐ Quackers™
  ("Quackers™"/wings)
  .... ❷ ❸ ❹ ❺
- ☐ Quackers™
  ("Quacker™"/no wings)
  ....❶ ❷
- ☐ Radar™.......... ❸ ❹

- ☐ Rainbow™
  (blue/no tongue)...... ❺
- ☐ Rex™ .... ❸
- ☐ Righty™ .... ❹
- ☐ Ringo™ .... ❸ ❹ ❺
- ☐ Roary™........... ❹ ❺
- ☐ Rover™........... ❹ ❺
- ☐ Santa™............ ❺
- ☐ Scoop™.......... ❹ ❺
- ☐ Scottie™.......... ❹ ❺
- ☐ Seamore™ ... ❶ ❷ ❸ ❹
- ☐ Seaweed™...... ❸ ❹ ❺
- ☐ Slither™........ ❶ ❷ ❸
- ☐ Sly™ (white belly).. ❹ ❺
- ☐ Sly™ (brown belly) .... ❹
- ☐ Snip™............ ❹ ❺
- ☐ Snort™........... ❹ ❺
- ☐ Snowball™......... ❹
- ☐ Sparky™ .... ❹
- ☐ Speedy™ .... ❶ ❷ ❸ ❹
- ☐ Spike™.......... ❹ ❺
- ☐ Spinner™ ("Spinner™"
  tush tag).......... ❹ ❺
- ☐ Spinner™ ("Creepy™"
  tush tag) .... ❺
- ☐ Splash™.... ❶ ❷ ❸ ❹
- ☐ Spooky™ ("Spooky™"
  swing tag)......... ❸ ❹
- ☐ Spooky™ ("Spook™"
  swing tag) .... ❸
- ☐ Spot™ (spot).... ❷ ❸ ❹
- ☐ Spot™ (no spot).... ❶ ❷
- ☐ Squealer™ ❶ ❷ ❸ ❹ ❺
- ☐ Steg™ .... ❸
- ☐ Sting™ .... ❸ ❹
- ☐ Stinger™ .... ❺
- ☐ Stinky™ .... ❸ ❹ ❺
- ☐ Stripes™ (light/
  fewer stripes) .... ❹ ❺
- ☐ Stripes™ (dark/
  fuzzy belly).......... ❸

❏ Stripes™ (dark/
more stripes) .... ❸
❏ Tabasco™ .... ❸ ❹
❏ Tank™
(9 plates/shell)....... ❹
❏ Tank™
(9 plates/no shell)..... ❹
❏ Tank™
(7 plates/no shell)..... ❸
❏ Teddy™ (brown/
new face) ...... ❷ ❸ ❹
❏ Teddy™ (brown/
old face)......... ❶ ❷
❏ Teddy™ (cranberry/
new face)........ ❷ ❸
❏ Teddy™ (cranberry/
old face)......... ❶ ❷
❏ Teddy™
(jade/new face) ... ❷ ❸
❏ Teddy™
(jade/old face).... ❶ ❷
❏ Teddy™ (magenta/
new face)........ ❷ ❸
❏ Teddy™ (magenta/
old face)......... ❶ ❷
❏ Teddy™
(teal/new face).... ❷ ❸
❏ Teddy™
(teal/old face) .... ❶ ❷
❏ Teddy™
(violet/new face).. ❷ ❸
❏ Teddy™
(violet/new face
employee bear w/red
tush tag)... **No Swing Tag**
❏ Teddy™
(violet/old face)... ❶ ❷
❏ Trap™ .... ❶ ❷ ❸
❏ Tuffy™............ ❹ ❺
❏ Tusk™
("Tusk™" swing tag) ❸ ❹
❏ Tusk™
("Tuck™" swing tag) ... ❹

❏ Twigs™ .... ❸ ❹ ❺
❏ Valentino™... ❷ ❸ ❹ ❺
❏ Velvet™ .... ❸ ❹
❏ Waddle™ ...... ❸ ❹ ❺
❏ Waves™ .... ❹ ❺
❏ Web™ .... ❶ ❷ ❸
❏ Weenie™ ...... ❸ ❹ ❺
❏ Wise™ .... ❺
❏ Wrinkles™ .... ❹ ❺
❏ Zero™ .... ❺
❏ Ziggy™ .... ❸ ❹ ❺
❏ Zip™ (white paws)❸ ❹ ❺
❏ Zip™ (all black) .... ❸
❏ Zip™ (white face).. ❷ ❸

Current Beanie Buddies®

❏ Beak™
❏ Bongo™
❏ Bubbles™
❏ Chilly™
❏ Chip™
❏ Erin™
❏ Hippity™
❏ Humphrey™
❏ Jake™
❏ Patti™
❏ Peanut™
❏ Peking™
❏ Pinky™
❏ Quackers™
❏ Rover™
❏ Smoochy™
❏ Snort™
❏ Squealer™
❏ Stretch™
❏ Teddy™
❏ Tracker™
❏ Waddle™
❏ Mystery Beanie
Buddies® Release

Retired Beanie Buddies®

❏ Twigs™

Retired Teenie Beanie Babies™

❏ 1997 Teenie Beanie
Babies™ Complete Set
❏ 1998 Teenie Beanie
Babies™ Complete Set
❏ Bones™
❏ Bongo™
❏ Chocolate™
❏ Chops™
❏ Doby™
❏ Goldie™
❏ Happy™
❏ Inch™
❏ Lizz™
❏ Mel™
❏ Patti™
❏ Peanut™
❏ Pinchers™
❏ Pinky™
❏ Quacks™
❏ Scoop™
❏ Seamore™
❏ Snort™
❏ Speedy™
❏ Twigs™
❏ Waddle™
❏ Zip™

collectible—anything and everything that is "able to be collected," including figurines, dolls, stamps, coins, memorabilia, etc. Even *bottle caps* can be considered a "collectible," but it is generally recognized that a true collectible should be something that increases in value over time.

current—a piece that is in production, although it may not be readily available in retail stores.

Info Beanie—a *Beanie Baby* character who is elected to narrate the *Beanie Babies'* daily activities through a diary found on the Ty web site. A new Info Beanie is chosen each month by collectors who visit the web site.

mint condition with both tags (MWBT)—piece offered on the secondary market in like-new condition with pristine swing and tush tags attached.

mistags—sometimes *Beanie Babies* will turn up with an incorrect swing or tush tag belonging to a different *Beanie Baby*. Tag errors are common and rarely affect a piece's value on the secondary market.

P.E. pellets—small, round pellets made of polyethylene used as fillings (the "beans") in many *Beanie Babies*.

P.V.C. pellets—small, round pellets made of polyvinyl chloride used as fillings (the "beans") in many *Beanie Babies*.

retired—a piece which is taken out of production, never to be made again. This is usually followed by a scarcity of the piece and a rise in value on the secondary market.

secondary market—the source for buying, selling and trading collectibles according to basic supply-and-demand principles. Popular pieces which have retired can appreciate in value far above the original issue price.

tag generation—style changes in the swing tags, which can help determine the approximate age of a *Beanie Baby*.

tush tag—folded fabric tag sewn into the seam near the bottom of *Beanie Babies*.

Tylon—a special fabric developed by Ty Warner himself for *Beanie Buddies*. This fabric is very soft and cool to the touch.

swing tag—the heart-shaped paper tag that comes attached to each *Beanie Baby*. This tag is attached by a small plastic strip, and is usually attached to the animal's left ear or head area.

variations—pieces that have color, design or printed text changes from the "original" piece.